Picnics

AND TAILGATE PARTIES

By the Editors
of
Sunset Books
and
Sunset Magazine

Lane Publishing Co. **∙** *Menlo Park, California*

Elegant simplicity—picnicking in style on foods gathered from the kitchen or a nearby market and packed in a roomy basket along with a few utensils. The basket's bounty includes salami, Camembert, crusty bread, a good wine, and seasonal fresh fruit to dip in honey.

Sunset goes on a picnic...

Is there anyone who doesn't like a picnic? For most people, the very idea conjures up visions of festive food enjoyed in good company at a favorite outdoor site. But the real beauty of picnicking is in its flexibility—for a picnic can be many different kinds of experiences. With our collection of imaginative picnic ideas, you can plan a romantic picnic for two or a festive tailgate party for a crowd, a lazy summer barbecue at the beach or high tea in a garden. You'll discover portable food ideas for holiday gatherings, and suggestions for spur-of-the-moment picnics inspired just by the fact that it's a beautiful day.

For contributing their knowledge and expertise, we extend special thanks to the staffs of the Village Cheese House and the Woodside Delicatessen. For sharing props used in our photographs, we thank Allied Arts Traditional Gift Shop; Beltramo's Liquors; Forrest Jones, Inc.; House of Today; S. Christian of Copenhagen; Taylor & Ng; Tunney Associates; Weber-Stephen Products; William Ober Co.; and Williams-Sonoma Kitchenware. And for her culinary assistance with our picnic photography, we thank Cynthia Scheer.

Special thanks to...

Proctor Mellquist, for his fifteen years of devoted persistence in urging us to publish this book.

Supervising Editor:
Cornelia Fogle

Staff Editors: **Claire Coleman**
Susan Warton

Contributing Editor: **Joan Griffiths**

Design: **Joe di Chiarro**
Cynthia Hanson

Photo Editor: **Lynne B. Morrall**

Illustrations: **Alan May**

Cover: Spanish Omelet Picnic Loaf (page 71) is a perfect outdoor entrée—it's sturdy and portable, needs little accompaniment to make a complete meal, and actually improves with standing as the zesty flavors of the omelet permeate the bread. A light red wine, assorted cheeses, and fresh fruit round out the menu. Photographed by Nikolay Zurek.

Photographers

Walter Georis: 2.   **Darrow M. Watt:** 18.
Tom Wyatt: 42.   **Nikolay Zurek:** 7, 10, 15, 23, 26, 31, 34, 39, 47, 50, 55, 58, 63, 67, 70, 75, 78, 83, 86, 91, 94.

Editor, Sunset Books: David E. Clark

First printing April 1982

Contents

Menus-on-the-Move

Choosing a theme and making it happen

What's a picnic? Strictly speaking, it's simply an outdoor meal. But to anyone who has ever indulged in one, a picnic is more than that—it's a special event, a festive occasion, even if it's a simple snack of bread and cheese in your own back yard.

Dedicated picnickers insist that there's a certain magic about sharing good food in the sunshine and fresh air. Perhaps it has to do with a more relaxed atmosphere outdoors; imaginative menu themes are easier to pull off when you're not sitting formally in a dining room. Or perhaps it's because picnicking is such a versatile art—a perfect vehicle for entertaining, for family outings, or for romantic, just-the-two-of-you getaways.

Our collection of picnic menus—with detailed instructions for preparing, transporting, and setting up the food—illustrates that picnicking can be whatever you want it to be: informal or decorous, close to home or far away, holiday-inspired or for no reason at all, except that it's a beautiful day.

Beach Barbecue

(Pictured on page 34)

Salt spray, sea air, warm sand underfoot—all these pleasant sensations of a day at the beach stir cravings for good and hearty food. Here's the perfect refreshment—a traditional beach-blanket banquet, complete with charcoal-grilled corn on the cob.

You can prepare this picnic to feed a crowd—or simply the family—on any summertime trip to the beach. For a small group, you may want to take only half the salad and leave the rest at home for a midweek supper.

Potato Chips

Crunchy Egg Dip (page 17)

Barbecued Hamburgers

French Rolls

Red Onion Slices

Tomato Slices   Lettuce

Barbecued Corn on the Cob (page 35)

Mixed Bean & Artichoke Salad (page 30)

Honey-Applesauce Cupcakes (page 77)

Soft Drinks   Beer

Bake the cupcakes on the day of the picnic—or bake them ahead and freeze them. If frozen, let the cupcakes thaw to room temperature on the morning of the outing.

Prepare the bean salad a day ahead and refrigerate it so the vegetables have time to marinate. Hard-cook the eggs for the salad garnish (if desired) and the egg dip at the same time.

On the morning of departure, slice the onions and tomatoes, and prepare the lettuce leaves; seal them in individual plastic bags or in small containers. Then prepare the egg dip and get the corn ready. Refrigerate the food that needs to be kept cold before packing it in the cooler.

Have ready one or more large bags of potato chips and enough hamburger patties and French rolls for your picnicking party. You'll also need a portable barbecue; potholders, a spatula, and tongs; and charcoal, charcoal starter, and fireplace matches.

Packing the picnic. Place chilled beer and soft drinks in the bottom of a roomy cooler. On top, pack the ears of corn and the egg dip. Tuck in the parcels containing the hamburger patties, garnishes for the salad, hamburger condiments, and butter for the corn.

Carry all the barbecue equipment in a sturdy box.

In a roomy basket, pack the unbreakable items first, including serving spoons for the salad, a bottle opener, salt and pepper, and a knife for the rolls (unless they're presliced). Fit in the cupcakes and the salad. Place the rolls and potato chips on top. For a sandy picnic, it's always wise to carry extra paper plates, napkins, and premoistened towelettes.

At the site. Start the charcoal about half an hour before you want to begin cooking; wait until the coals turn gray before grilling the meat and corn. Meanwhile, spread the blanket and let people nibble on potato chips with dip.

If your site is very sandy or some of the guests are quite young, you may prefer to wait until the hamburgers and corn are almost ready before you unpack the rest of the food. Before serving the salad, stir it well; then garnish it with the egg slices, if desired, and artichokes.

Guatemalan Appetizer Party

(Pictured on page 23)

Put a little Latin sparkle into those long days of summer with this Guatemalan fiesta of fabulous food. Enough boquitas, or "little mouthfuls," can make a whole meal and create a colorful focus for the picnic as guests pile up their own bite-size morsels, as mild or hot as they please. Our own favorite combinations are cabbage and carrot slaw on shredded pork, topped with guacamole; radishes on shredded pork with a squeeze of lime; and shredded pork with black beans.

Since at least 10 tiny dishes go into boquitas, this menu travels more easily to the patio than to a more remote picnic site. But if you do choose to transport it away from home, take along a portable table if the site won't provide one—everything tips easily, and most of this meal is finger food.

Boquitas (page 22)

Fresh Fruit

Guatemalan Sugar Cookies (page 73)

Beer   Cider

To get a head start, you can bake the cookies in advance and freeze them; they're very fragile, so pack them with care in freezer containers. Or bake the cookies a day or two ahead and store them in an airtight container.

A day ahead, prepare the pork, salsa, slaw, and beans. Refrigerate them separately until the next day. For convenience, you may want to purchase the potato salad (a pint is enough) and the guacamole, along with the other purchased menu items.

(Continued on next page)

On the morning of the picnic, reheat the pork and the black beans. While they're warming, shred the cheese (we served jack), slice the radishes, and fry the tortilla rounds.

Packing the picnic. Pack each boquita item (except the hot ones) in an individual plastic bowl or container with a tight-fitting lid. Wrap the hot pans containing the black beans and the pork according to the directions on page 90.

Load the beer and cider into the cooler first. Around the beverages, tuck in the fruit (we took apricots, mangoes, grapes, watermelon, and bananas). Also pack the salsa, salads, cheeses, radishes, beets, guacamole, and limes.

The tortilla rounds and cookies can travel in another picnic carrier, along with a knife for the fruit, premoistened towelettes, potholders, and plates, forks, and extra napkins in case guests overload their boquitas. You'll also need a serving spoon for each boquita dish.

At the site. You can transfer the hot foods to small dishes or serve directly from the pots. Set out bowls of the other boquita ingredients, stand back, and watch the stacks mount!

Pocket Bread Banquet

(Pictured on page 7)

As if designed especially for picnic convenience, pocket bread holds its filling in a tidy little single-serving pouch. When the filling is spicy and succulent lamb shish kebabs, this simple Middle Eastern sandwich bread becomes a magnificent meal in itself.

Embellish each serving of lamb with fresh vegetables, a dash of chutney, and a dollop of minty yogurt. To complete a memorable banquet for six to eight, all you need add are a basket of fruit, some nut-laced cookies, a light red wine, and some sparkling cider.

Barbecued Lamb in Pocket Bread (page 65)

Chutney   Sliced Cucumbers

Romaine Spears

Tomato Wedges

Yogurt with Chopped Fresh Mint and Cucumbers

Fresh Fruit

Walnut Jewel Cookies (page 73)

Filbert Crescents (page 76)

California Gamay

Sparkling Cider

Coffee

Bake the cookies ahead of time and freeze them; or bake them the day before the picnic. They travel well in a large, heavy bowl, covered with plastic wrap.

You can barbecue the lamb at home or at the picnic site; plan the marinating time (about 3 hours) accordingly. Have ready an assortment of seasonal fruit. Either purchase the pocket bread or make your own, as we did.

Packing the picnic. Carefully set the bottles of cider in the bottom of a cooler. On top, arrange individual containers filled with the tomato wedges,

romaine spears, cucumber slices, and marinated onion rings. Take the yogurt separately from the chopped mint and cucumber; combine them just before serving. Add to the cooler any fruit you want to keep cold, the chutney, and cream for the coffee.

If you're not grilling the lamb at home, pack the container of marinating lamb in the cooler. For barbecuing, you'll also need charcoal, charcoal starter, potholders, tongs, fireplace matches, sturdy metal skewers—and, if there are no cooking facilities at the site, a portable barbecue.

To take hot shish kebabs, wrap them in foil and carry them as directed on page 90. Tuck the foil-wrapped package of warmed pocket bread in with the lamb.

Pour hot coffee into two preheated thermoses (see page 90) and pack them, along with the wine, in a roomy basket or hamper. Add the unbreakable items next, remembering a platter for the lamb, serving forks and spoons for the condiments, a multipurpose bottle opener, a corkscrew, and sugar for the coffee.

Since the sandwiches are hand-held, include plenty of extra napkins and some premoistened towelettes. Last of all, pack the fragile items, including the pocket bread (unless heated).

At the site. To barbecue, light the coals about half an hour before you want to begin cooking. Add the skewers of lamb when the coals are gray; warm the pocket bread for about 10 minutes. When you're almost ready to serve, combine the yogurt with the mint and cucumber, tear or cut the bread rounds in half, and set out the condiments. Offer the fruit and two kinds of cookies for a sweet ending.

Pocket Bread Banquet

Much of this lavish spread gets neatly tucked inside halves of pita to make Barbecued Lamb in Pocket Bread (page 65). Spicy marinated lamb cubes and onion rings contrast with the refreshing coolness of the other vegetables and the mint-flavored yogurt topping. For an easy-to-eat finale, a brimming bowlful of crunchy nut cookies—sugar-dusted Filbert Crescents (page 76) and Walnut Jewel Cookies (page 73) glistening with dots of red currant jelly.

Provençal Picnic

(Pictured on page 31)

From the farms and kitchens of Provence, in southern France, come some of the world's most lively flavors—celebrated here in a picnic fit for a Sunday drive through the Provençal countryside.

This most elegant meal-in-a-basket would provide memorable outdoor dining at a summer concert or other special open-air occasion. The menu serves six.

Tomato Tarts Niçoise (page 59)

Green Bean & Red Pepper Salad (page 30)

Niçoise Olives

Cheeses   Baguettes

Pine Nut Tarts (page 82)

Cherries

French Tavel Rosé or California Zinfandel Blanc

Stored airtight at room temperature, the dessert tarts keep so well that you can bake them up to a week in advance.

For most attractive presentation, assemble and toss the salad at the picnic site. But cook the beans and marinate the peppers ahead of time, keeping them in the refrigerator until you're ready to leave. The beans can travel in a plastic bag, the pepper strips in their container.

Bake the tomato tarts close to departure time. Arrange them on a rimmed tray that will fit inside your cooler.

Buy the Niçoise olives at a delicatessen—or substitute ripe olives. Have ready two or three baguettes; you'll enjoy slices of these long, crusty loaves with the cheese. We took Camembert and three French goat cheeses—*fromage de chèvre* and two batons of *chevrette*.

Packing the picnic. Nestle the wine into a cooler, with beans, olives, peppers, lettuce, and cherries. In a box or basket, pack the unbreakable items first; place the fragile wine glasses (wrapped in napkins), cheeses, baguettes, and entrée and dessert tarts on top. Don't forget a bowl and serving spoon for the salad, bread and cheese knives, a fork for the olives, and a corkscrew.

At the site. Gently combine the beans with the marinated pepper strips and arrange them in a bowl lined with lettuce leaves. The tomato tarts can be eaten out of hand, but you'll want to provide plates and forks for the salad.

Romantic Picnic for Two

(Pictured on page 55)

Cupid couldn't have planned a more lyrical lunch for two. Delicate chilled salmon, accented with fresh, first-of-the-season asparagus, sets a delicious springtime mood—especially when presented on a pretty cloth in some quiet, leafy glade.

Sharing the scene with the entrée are butter-tender croissants, dainty raspberry tarts, and cold, bubbly champagne.

Poached Salmon Steaks with Asparagus (page 53) and Green Butter Mayonnaise

Croissants   Butter Curls

Fresh Raspberry Barquettes (page 84)

Blanc de Noir California Champagne

Cook the salmon and asparagus the day before the picnic, and let them chill overnight in the refrigerator. You can prepare the mayonnaise and the raspberry barquettes at the same time, or wait until the next morning.

Using firm butter and a butter curler or vegetable peeler, make the butter curls well in advance so they can chill thoroughly. For perfect freshness, buy the croissants en route; or buy them in advance and freeze immediately, then take them out to thaw on the morning of the picnic.

Packing the picnic. Carry each small item—the mayonnaise, the butter, and the garnishes for the salmon—in an individual container. If your cooler is roomy enough to hold the plates side by side, you can arrange the cold salmon and asparagus (but not the garnishes) on plates and wrap them securely in plastic wrap. Otherwise, carry the salmon and asparagus in individual foil packets and assemble the plates at the picnic site.

Place the prechilled champagne on the bottom of the cooler; flank it with the small containers of mayonnaise, butter, and garnishes. Fill any gaps with plastic bags of ice cubes (needed later for the improvised champagne bucket); try to create a fairly level surface for the plates of salmon and asparagus. Place the plates on top and surround them with more bags of ice cubes.

In a basket, place the cutlery, including a spoon for the mayonnaise and a tiny fork for the butter curls. Wrap the wine glasses in cloth napkins and tuck them in; add the folded picnic cloth to keep all secure.

Protecting them with paper towels, pack the luncheon plates (if not carried in the cooler) and dessert plates in a second basket, along with plates or small baskets for the croissants and the barquettes. Set the delicate baked goods on top—the croissants in a plastic bag, the barquettes in a pan or box.

At the site. After spreading the cloth, assemble the salmon and asparagus (if not done ahead) and garnish each serving. Place the bags of ice cubes in one of the emptied baskets to simulate a champagne bucket. Then set out the rest of the food, pop the champagne cork . . . and have a lovely time.

Nomads' Feast

(Pictured on page 47)

Borrowed from the Bedouins, this lamb and rice feast is just one example of the portable meals enjoyed by those nomadic people who picnic on the sand every night of the week.

Invite six or seven hungry friends to your favorite picnic spot or simply set out the banquet on a blanket or rug on the patio at home. Clusters of cushions will help create a Middle Eastern mood, as well as adding to everyone's comfort during the meal.

Cucumber Cream Soup
(page 25)
Mansef (page 48)
Pistachio Nuts
Fresh Fruit
Almond Cake (page 77)
Turkish Coffee

A day ahead of the picnic, bake the cake. When it's cool, score it diagonally into diamond-shaped pieces and cover

the pan with foil or plastic wrap. Prepare the soup and refrigerate it until the next day.

You can cook the mansef (but not the rice) a day ahead or on the morning of the picnic. Brown the pine nuts when you cook the meat and pack them in a jar or plastic bag.

About an hour before departure time, reheat the lamb in its Dutch oven over low heat for about 40 minutes, stirring occasionally. Prepare the rice and warm the foil-wrapped tortillas. Fill a preheated thermos with Turkish coffee.

Before pouring the soup into prechilled thermoses, taste it and season again, if necessary. (For preheating and prechilling instructions, see page 90.)

Packing the picnic. Wrap and transport the hot dishes— the rice (with foil-wrapped tortillas inside the pot) and the mansef—according to the directions on page 90.

In a large basket or hamper, pack a serving spoon and wide serving platter, plates for dessert (include some extra ones for any mansef eaters who prefer not to eat out of hand), cups for both soup and coffee, a few forks and spoons, plenty of napkins, the thermoses of soup, meat juice, and coffee, and a knife and cutting board for the fruit.

In nooks, tuck in pistachio nuts, pine nuts, and garnishes for the mansef. If you want to garnish the soup, include some

chopped fresh mint and shelled sunflower seeds. Add the fruit; if there's room, set the cake pan on top.

At the site. Garnish the soup, if you like, and serve it in cups. To assemble the mansef, spoon hot rice onto the platter and spoon mansef over it. Pour some of the hot meat juices over the meat and sprinkle pine nuts on top. Arrange folded tortillas around the rim of the platter and garnish with lemon wedges and sprigs of mint. Keep the mansef hot by pouring on more of the hot juices as needed.

To eat, guests spoon the mansef mixture onto a tortilla, add a squeeze of lemon, then refold and eat out of hand. For dessert, arrange diamonds of cake on a plate and slice the fruit. Pass around steaming cups of coffee.

Hearty Dutch Oven Picnic

(Pictured on page 58)

In brisk and bracing weather, picnickers get hungry for hearty fare. Here's sustenance, ample and tasty, for eight to ten robust appetites.

The spicy beef sandwich filling travels easily in the perfect winter's day picnic pot— a big (6 to 8-quart) Dutch oven with a tight-fitting lid to prevent spills. Properly wrapped, the pot—whether made of cast iron, aluminum, or pottery— stays hot for up to 4 hours.

Barbecued Beef Sandwiches
(page 43)
Assorted Raw Vegetables
Best Chocolate Chip Cookies
(page 74)
Beer   Hot Coffee

(Continued on page 11)

Breakfast on the Road

Setting out on a jaunt that requires an early-morning departure? Rather than taking time for breakfast at home, prepare a picnic you can enjoy along the way or once you reach your destination. Pastry-wrapped Sausages (page 68)—cooked sausage links enveloped in puff pastry—are the heart of this picnic. Eat them like sandwiches, accompanied by fruit, cheese, simple sweets, and coffee.

. . . Hearty Dutch Oven Picnic (cont'd.)

If it's most convenient, you can bake and freeze the cookies well ahead of time; thaw them the morning of the picnic. Also have very fresh sandwich buns ready; we took onion rolls, but poppy seed rolls or seeded hamburger buns are fine, too.

Cook the beef a day or two ahead; about 2 hours before departing, reheat the sliced beef in its thick sauce. If you like, you can wrap the rolls in foil and heat them in the same oven for about 15 minutes. When the beef filling is bubbly hot, wrap the Dutch oven as directed on page 90.

Packing the picnic. Carry the pot in a carton or insulated bag; tuck the rolls alongside. If there's still room in the carton, add the coffee—you'll need two preheated thermoses (see page 90).

Pack the beer in the bottom of a cooler. On top, put plastic bags filled with raw vegetables (we took carrots, celery, zucchini, and cherry tomatoes). Tuck in cream for the coffee, too.

Stack the cookies in a box or tin; then pack them, along with sugar for the coffee, in a basket or hamper. Add serving paraphernalia, including potholders, a large spoon for the beef, and a knife for the rolls. Since the sandwiches can be drippy, it's a good idea to take along knives, forks, and plates.

At the site. When you're ready to eat, just split the rolls and spoon on the hot meat and sauce.

Alfresco Italian Lunch

(Pictured on page 70)

Throughout the year, the weather smiles so benignly in much of Italy that dining *alfresco* (literally "in the fresh") is a pleasure of everyday life.

Celebrating the exuberant spirit of such feasting, the following menu turns any afternoon into a spur-of-the-moment Italian holiday. We served from a back yard picnic table—but apart from the espresso pot, everything travels farther afield with no problem. There's plenty for four people.

**Pizza Focaccia Sandwiches
(page 61)
Crumb Cooky (page 73)
Persian Melon or Cantaloupe
Fresh Figs
Chianti   Bottled Water
Espresso**

Make the focaccia as far ahead as is convenient. It keeps in the refrigerator for up to 2 days, much longer if frozen. Let the bread come to room temperature before the picnic; then simply carry it in its foil wrapping. Have ready the meats, cheese, and cut-up vegetables for toppings.

You'll need to bake the Italian cooky a full day ahead of the event so it has time to age. Since you'll break it apart to serve, there's no need to take pains to protect it during transport; just pop it into a large plastic bag or wrap it in foil.

Packing the picnic. Carry the sandwich toppings in a cooler, along with the Chianti and bottled water.

Pack a roomy basket or hamper with the unbreakable items first. You'll need a preheated thermos of espresso and serving dishes. Include forks for the sandwich makings, a knife for the melon, and a corkscrew. Tuck in the fruit, the cooky, and the focaccia.

At the site. Arrange the sandwich toppings on serving dishes. Set out the focaccia, slice the fruit, arrange big chunks of cooky in a bowl— and let guests help themselves.

Fourth of July Potluck Supper

(Pictured on page 91)

Skyrocketing on the perfect-day-for-a-picnic poll, the Fourth of July is one occasion when far more Americans dine outdoors than in.

To celebrate this star-spangled holiday, we've organized a feast of some of America's favorites—from fried chicken to chocolate cake, cheeseburgers to homemade strawberry ice cream. Divide it among three or four families for a sparkling potluck supper in the park before the fireworks begin.

**Parsley Potato Salad
(page 32)
Mushroom-Artichoke Salad
(page 29)
Chile-spiced Bean Salad
(page 32)
Crusty Parmesan Chicken
(page 51)
Deviled Eggs
Pickled Beets
Barbecued Cheeseburgers
Tomatoes   Radishes   Lettuce
Red Onions   Pickles   Olives
Chocolate Buttercream Cake
(page 82)
Strawberry Ice Cream
(page 85)
Strawberries
Beer   Lemonade   Coffee**

Divide the menu as you see fit. For an easy division among four families, have one bring all three salads; have a second family in charge of the chicken (double or triple the recipe),

... **Potluck Supper** (cont'd.)

deviled eggs, and assorted vegetables; let a third family provide a portable barbecue (if you can't count on park facilities), hamburgers, buns, cheese, condiments, and barbecuing equipment (charcoal, starter, fireplace matches, potholders, spatula, and tongs).

The fourth family tops off the picnic with the beverages and desserts—the cake and the ice cream, along with a hand-crank freezer, rock salt, and lots of ice.

Packing the picnic. It's easiest to have each family bring its own plates, cups, cutlery, napkins, and tablecloth.

The salads can be prepared a day in advance. It's probably not necessary to double the recipes unless the families are large, since people will probably take small samples of each. Be sure to include a serving spoon for each salad.

The Parmesan chicken can be served cold or warm. Either bake it a day ahead, refrigerate it, and carry it in a cooler; or pop it in the oven about an hour before you leave and transport it hot as directed on page 90. The deviled eggs can be made from your favorite recipe or from one of those on page 36; they need several hours to chill and must be packed in a cooler, along with the assortment of vegetables (each in a plastic container). Take along a basket or platter for the chicken, a tray for the eggs, and serving forks.

All the barbecue equipment can travel in a sturdy cardboard box; if there's room, lay the buns and cheese on top so they don't get squished. The hamburgers and condiments should be packed in a cooler.

The dessert chef can bake the cake and prepare the frosting well in advance; both can be stored in the freezer. After thawing, the frosting should be beaten for a few minutes with an electric mixer. A round plastic serving plate with a high, tight-fitting cover is ideal for transporting the cake; remember to carry along a knife and a cake server.

In a cooler, pack the ice cream custard, berry mixture, and ice, each in its own container. Take a hammer and large, heavy dishtowel for crushing ice cubes, and rock salt for the ice cream freezer. Pack the fragile ice cream cones and berries for garnish last.

Keep the beer in the cooler. For the lemonade and coffee, you'll need a couple of thermoses. Preheat the one for the coffee; don't forget to take cream (kept cold) and sugar. Prechill the other thermos and fill it with cold lemonade. (For preheating and prechilling instructions, see page 90.)

At the site. When enough helpers have gathered, assemble the ice cream freezer and begin hand-cranking, taking turns so that everyone can participate. If the ice cream is ready before it's time for dessert, remove the dasher, cover the container, and let it stay in the freezer to ripen; don't forget to dump out the salty water and pack the freezer with fresh ice.

Fire up the barbecue about 30 minutes before you want to begin cooking. Grill the cheeseburgers when the coals are gray. Arrange the chicken in a basket, set out the rest of the food, and dig in.

French Country Picnic

(Pictured on page 78)

So appreciative are they of a glorious meal—and what's more glorious than to dine outdoors?—that it's no surprise the French enjoy *pique-niques.*

This one starts with a country version of classic pâté. The feasting moves along to exquisitely herbed roast chicken, served with a rich vegetable stew, and ends with elegant fruit tart for dessert. Serve a slightly chilled dry white wine to complete this menu, designed for six to eight people.

Country-style Pâté (page 19)
Cornichons   Butter Lettuce
Baguettes   Sweet Butter
Ratatouille (page 36)
**Roast Chicken with Herbs
(page 49)**
**Brandied Apricot Tart
(page 84)**
Pinot Chardonnay

To bring out their rich flavors, prepare both the pâté and the ratatouille at least a day ahead. You'll also need to roast the chickens in advance so they'll be well chilled by the time you're ready to leave.

Bake the tart on the morning of the picnic or a day in advance. Also have ready two or three very fresh baguettes.

Packing the picnic. In a cooler, stow the wine, butter, pâté (in its dish), lettuce leaves, and chickens.

In a basket or hamper, pack the unbreakable items first. Be sure to include a server for the pâté and the tart and a serving spoon for the ratatouille, plus a bread knife, a tiny fork for the cornichons, a

(Continued on page 14)

Impromptu Picnics

A picnic doesn't have to be a big production planned far ahead of time. Instead, it can be a spur-of-the-moment affair on an unexpectedly sunny day, or a brown-bag break from the school or workday routine.

Ingredients may require a little high-speed assembly in the kitchen before departure, or they may come ready to eat from a delicatessen or supermarket, or even from your pantry shelf. You'll probably be able to keep equipment to a minimum—most picnics of this type require only such basics as a multipurpose can and bottle opener or Swiss Army knife, plastic eating utensils, and perhaps small salt and pepper shakers.

Remember that the key ideas here are ease and spontaneity. You don't need to carry a lot of food or travel a long distance. In fact, you don't even have to be outdoors—if you use your imagination and stretch a point, you can just as easily arrange the food on a desk or drawing board and declare it a picnic!

Here are some appealing themes for quick picnicking; all of them can easily be adapted to accommodate what you find in the market or have in the house.

Desk Drawer Special

Deviled Ham or Canned Pâté
Canned Cheese (Camembert or Brie)
Melba Toast
Marinated Artichoke Hearts
Packaged Cookies
Split of Red Wine

Designed to be kept in a drawer until mealtime, this elegant, nonperishable picnic is perfect for those times when eating may be delayed, or when refrigeration isn't available. All the ingredients can be purchased ahead of time and stored indefinitely; they can also easily feed two. Just make sure you have a can

opener and knife in the drawer along with the food.

Brown-Bag Smörgasbord

Buttered Pumpernickel Slices
Kipper Snacks or Brisling Sardines
Cucumber and Raw Mushroom Slices
Green Pepper Strips or Onion Rings
Cheese
Dried Apricots
Canned Fruit or Vegetable Juice

This Scandinavian-inspired picnic requires a little at-home preparation—butter the bread and package it, buttered sides together; also, cut the vegetables and wrap them well. Choose a Scandinavian cheese, such as a creamy Havarti, lappi, or Danish fontina. At lunchtime, top each bread slice with fish and vegetables as desired.

Shop-and-Serve Picnic

Barbecued Chicken
French Bread   Butter
Coleslaw
Fresh Fruit
Fontinella Cheese
Chilled White Wine

With picnic food that's purchased right before the event, you can enjoy hot barbecued chicken and chilled wine without worrying about insulated packing. A delicatessen or supermarket with a rotisserie can provide what you need. If you're picnicking with a group, allow half a medium-size chicken and 2 ounces of cheese per serving, and enough bread, coleslaw, fruit, and wine to satisfy everyone's appetite.

small butter spreader, a cork-screw, and poultry shears for cutting up the chicken. You'll need a serving platter for the chicken, too.

Both the ratatouille and the cornichons can travel in the basket. Carefully wrap the tart (in its pan) and place it in a snug-fitting box for protection; lay the box and the baguettes on top of the basket.

At the site. To serve the pâté as a first course, make little open-faced sandwiches by stacking a slice of buttered bread with a lettuce leaf, thick slice of pâté, and a cornichon. Then spread out the banquet buffet-style. Bon appétit!

Indian Summer Picnic

(Pictured on page 39)

One of our favorites, this menu features foods that are entirely make-ahead, easy to pack, and free of last-minute fuss. And the flavors—from hearty, chilled meat loaf studded with pine nuts to crisp, red September apples—blend in mellow harmony, perfectly in tune with the delicious golden days of Indian summer.

A plentiful spread, this picnic provides enough food for 12 to 14 people. Invite family and friends to enjoy the last lazy days of warm weather—or the first splendor of autumn.

Casserole Meat Loaf (page 44)

Garden Vegetable Salad Bowl (page 29)

French Bread   Butter

Crisp Red Apples

Cheesecake Cookies (page 74)

Red Jug Wine

Iced or Hot Coffee

You can bake the cheesecake cookies (double the recipe) well in advance, then freeze them. Before leaving home, cut them into bars and cover the baking pan with foil.

Prepare the meat loaf a day in advance of the picnic, then refrigerate it so it will be well chilled for the next day. Cook and marinate the salad vegetables (again, double the ingredients) on the evening or early morning before departure—they need at least 4 hours in the refrigerator. You can toss to mix at the picnic site.

Have ready a loaf or two of very fresh French bread, and a dozen or more crisp apples.

For a hot beverage, fill two preheated thermoses with hot coffee. For iced coffee, fill chilled thermoses with cold coffee. (See page 90 for pre-heating and prechilling instructions.)

Packing the picnic. Carry the meat loaf in its casserole, wrapped in foil or plastic wrap. Pack it snugly in a cooler and place the apples around it. Add the pan of cookies, a stick of butter for the sandwiches, and cream for the coffee.

In a basket, take along the salad in a covered bowl, a bread knife and cutting board, plates, forks and butter knives, serving utensils for the salad and meat loaf, and a small spatula for lifting out the bar cookies. Don't forget sugar for the coffee. Pack the unbreak-able items first, the French bread last of all.

At the site. About half an hour before you're ready to eat, mix the salad. To serve the meat loaf, cut ½-inch-thick slices and offer with bread (buttered, if desired) for sandwiches. At dessert time, lift the cookies out of their pan with the spatula; eat either out of hand or with forks and plates.

Grandstand Picnic

(Pictured on page 67)

When a youngster in the family takes to soccer or softball, everyone else usually takes to the bleachers. And as every sports fan knows, the excite-ment of cheering from the sidelines builds a ravenous hunger in no time at all.

Here's hearty appeasement in a delicious and easily por-table lunch for a family of four (keep the athlete's portion in the cooler for later on).

Carrot Soup (page 22) with Jumbo Croutons

Roast Beef & Spinach Pinwheels (page 66)

Fresh Strawberries

Packaged Cookies

Red Wine   Lemonade

A day ahead of the game, pre-pare the soup and refrigerate it overnight. You can make the croutons at the same time; store them separately in a covered container. The next day, make the pinwheel and chill it for a few hours. Have ready a bas-ket of strawberries and a box of the family's favorite cookies.

Packing the picnic. In a basket stow the wine, lemonade in a prechilled thermos (see page 90), croutons, and cookies, along with a corkscrew, a knife and board for cutting the pinwheel, and cups for the soup. Take along soup spoons if you're serving the croutons. Pack the wrapped pinwheel (uncut), chopped parsley, and strawberries in a cooler.

At the site. Offer cups of parsley-garnished soup with croutons. Then slice the pin-wheel. Pass strawberries and cookies for dessert.

Pedalers' Picnic

Cyclists and other travelers needn't let limited carrying space prevent them from enjoying a quick, high-energy meal on the road. Papaya, yogurt, lime, and canned turkey for the Papaya Turkey Salad (page 51), as well as packaged smoked almonds and canned fruit drinks, can be purchased at a supermarket along the route. With a few utensils from home, and a scenic spot, riders can enjoy a refreshing pause.

Appetite Enhancers

Set the stage with tempting appetizers and savory soups

What to serve for outdoor openers? It's a problem you'll enjoy solving with the recipes for appetizers and soups in this chapter.

Appetizers for outdoor enjoyment range from simple dips to pâtés, terrines,

homemade gravlax, and clams that pop open on the barbecue. Choose your favorite, depending on your menu and how much time you want to spend in preparation.

For maximum pleasure with minimum effort, consider cheeses (page 24) as hors d'oeuvres; they're traditional picnicking favorites.

Soups are also an effective and delicious way to whet the appetite. Hot or cold, chunky or smooth, they travel conveniently in thermoses and

complement any menu. We've even included a versatile fruit soup that can accompany an outdoor breakfast or be served with cookies for dessert.

When preparing cold soups, remember that they thicken when chilled and lose some of the assertiveness of their seasonings; be sure to taste before pouring the soup into the thermos, and make adjustments, if necessary.

Cherry Tomatoes in Herb Marinade

Though it sounds like a lot of work, peeling cherry tomatoes isn't hard, and is worth the effort to create these piquant appetizers. At the picnic, you can eat them with picks directly from the serving container.

2 baskets cherry tomatoes
  Boiling water
¼ cup red wine vinegar
2 green onions (including tops), sliced
½ teaspoon dry basil
¼ teaspoon oregano leaves
1 teaspoon garlic salt
¼ teaspoon pepper
½ cup salad oil (may be part olive oil)

Place tomatoes, a few at a time, in a wire strainer and immerse in a large pan of rapidly boiling water for about 15 seconds. Immediately rinse tomatoes under cold water. Slip off and discard peels and stems, and place tomatoes in a shallow container with a tight-fitting lid.

In a small bowl, combine vinegar, onions, basil, oregano, garlic salt, pepper, and oil; beat well, then pour over tomatoes. Cover and refrigerate for at least 2 hours or until next day, stirring several times.

To serve, eat with wooden picks directly from container, or spoon tomatoes onto plates. Makes 6 servings.

Avocado Vegetable Dip

(Pictured on page 26)

Laced with chopped vegetables and zapped with a touch of liquid hot pepper seasoning, this creamy avocado dip goes well with tortilla chips or crisp raw vegetables.

2 large ripe avocados
2 tablespoons lime or lemon juice
1 package (.6 oz.) Italian or Caesar salad dressing mix
½ cup sour cream
1 carrot, shredded
2 green onions (including tops), finely chopped
½ cup *each* finely chopped broccoli, cauliflower, and celery
¼ teaspoon liquid hot pepper seasoning
  Salt

Peel, pit, and mash avocados. Place in a bowl and stir in lime juice and dry dressing mix. Add sour cream, carrot, onions, broccoli, cauliflower, celery, hot pepper seasoning, and salt to taste; stir well. Cover and refrigerate for at least 2 hours or until next day. Transport in a cooler. Makes 4 cups.

Crunchy Egg Dip

(Pictured on page 34)

Bacon and eggs are more than just a breakfast staple; here they combine with cream cheese and crunchy vegetables to make a tempting dip.

1 large package (8 oz.) cream cheese, softened
4 hard-cooked eggs, finely chopped
4 strips bacon, crisply cooked, drained, and crumbled
1 small dill pickle, chopped
½ medium-size green pepper, seeded and chopped
½ cup thinly sliced green onions (including tops)
1 tablespoon milk
  Salt and pepper

In a medium-size bowl, stir together cheese, eggs, bacon, pickle, green pepper, and onions until well combined. Stir in milk and season to taste with salt and pepper. Cover and refrigerate for at least 2 hours or until next day. Transport in a cooler. Makes about 3 cups.

Cheese Twists

(Pictured on page 83)

Flaky golden cheese twists make an attractive and tempting picnic hors d'oeuvre. Serve them at brunch, lunch, or dinner—they'll disappear quickly no matter what the time of day.

¾ cup all-purpose flour
½ cup shredded Cheddar cheese
⅛ teaspoon ground red pepper (cayenne)
4 tablespoons butter or margarine
1 egg yolk beaten with 2 tablespoons water

In a medium-size bowl, stir together flour, cheese, and red pepper. With a pastry blender or 2 knives, cut butter into flour mixture until it resembles fine crumbs. Stir in egg yolk mixture. Gather dough into a ball, dust with flour, wrap, and refrigerate until firm.

On a lightly floured board, roll out dough ¼ inch thick. With a floured knife, cut dough into strips ½ inch wide and 3 to 4 inches long. Holding ends of each strip, twist in opposite directions. Place twists slightly apart on ungreased baking sheets. If dough or twists become soft, refrigerate until firm. (At this point, you may freeze twists on baking sheets; when twists are firm, remove from baking sheets, package airtight, and return to freezer.)

(Continued on page 19)

Backyard Birthday Party

Turning five is full of fun at an outdoor birthday party with plenty of kid-pleasing food. Children will love Alphabet Vegetable Soup (page 27) and frothy Banana Fruit Slush (page 80); they'll be surprised to find juicy frankfurters nestled in the Potato Pups (page 68) under a generous serving of mustard-spiked potato salad. And what child can't find just a bit of room for Cut-out Sugar Cookies (page 74) for dessert!

Bake in a 400° oven for about 10 minutes (about 14 minutes, if frozen) or until golden. Let cool on racks; transport in a covered container. Makes about 2 dozen.

Pop-open Barbecue Clams

Placed on a hot grill, tightly closed clam shells pop open to reveal their juicy contents.

4 dozen small hard-shell clams
6 tablespoons butter or margarine
Crusty bread or rolls

Scrub clams thoroughly with a stiff-bristled brush under cold running water. Transport clams and butter in a cooler.

At picnic site, melt butter in a small pan on a grill 3 to 5 inches above a solid bed of glowing coals. Push to a cool corner.

Set clams on grill and cook until they begin to open (about 3 minutes); turn clams over and continue to cook until they pop wide open.

Protecting your fingers with a napkin, pick up a hot clam shell and drain juices into pan with butter. Then pluck out clam meat with a fork, dip in butter, and eat. When clams are gone, dunk bits of bread into clam-flavored butter. Makes 6 servings.

Gravlax

The delicate salmon appetizer the Swedes call *gravlax* is finest when made with the freshest salmon you can find. A dill-seasoned mixture of salt and sugar cures and firms the fish; when finished, it resembles delicatessen lox.

1 teaspoon *each* dill weed and dill seeds, or 1 tablespoon finely chopped fresh dill
2 tablespoons salt
¼ cup sugar
12 black peppercorns
1 or 2 skinless center-section salmon fillets (about 2 lbs. *total*)
Sweet Mustard Sauce (recipe follows)
Pumpernickel or rye bread

In a small bowl, mix dill weed, dill seeds, salt, sugar, and peppercorns. Rub mixture onto salmon. Place fish in a rimmed, flat-bottomed dish that fits salmon compactly. Cover and refrigerate until next day, basting occasionally.

Prepare Sweet Mustard Sauce and pour into a container; cover tightly and set aside. Discard brine and cut fish across the grain into thin, slanting slices. Wrap in plastic wrap. If made ahead, refrigerate for up to a week.

Transport fish in a cooler. Serve on bread and top with sauce. Makes 8 to 12 servings.

Sweet Mustard Sauce. In a small bowl, stir together 2 tablespoons **Dijon mustard**, 1 tablespoon **sugar**, 1½ tablespoons **white wine vinegar**, ½ teaspoon **salt**, and 1 teaspoon finely chopped **fresh dill** or ¼ teaspoon dill weed. With a fork, gradually and smoothly beat in ⅓ cup **salad oil.** Makes about ⅔ cup.

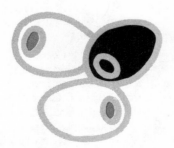

Country-style Pâté

(Pictured on page 78)

This rich, well-seasoned pâté of ground meats and liver tastes even better after the seasonings are allowed to mingle for a day or two. Refrigerated, it keeps for up to a week. Serve it with *cornichons* or gherkin pickles.

6 strips bacon
2 tablespoons butter or margarine
2 medium-size onions, finely chopped
¼ cup brandy
¾ pound boneless veal stew meat or ground veal
¾ pound boneless pork shoulder or ground pork
¼ pound pork fat
¼ pound chicken or beef liver
2 eggs
5 cloves garlic, minced or pressed
2 teaspoons salt
1½ teaspoons *each* ground sage and pepper
1 teaspoon thyme leaves
¼ teaspoon *each* ground cloves, ground allspice, and ground nutmeg
2 bay leaves

Place bacon in a wide frying pan and cover with water. Cover pan and simmer over low heat for 10 minutes. Drain bacon and pat dry. Set aside.

In a small pan over medium heat, melt butter. Add onions and cook, stirring occasionally, until soft (about 10 minutes). Add brandy and cook for 2 more minutes. Remove from heat and set aside.

Using a food chopper or food processor, grind veal and pork (if not purchased ground), fat, and liver. Turn into a large bowl and combine with onion mixture, eggs, garlic, salt, sage, pepper, thyme, cloves, allspice, and nutmeg.

(Continued on next page)

Protecting Foods from Spoilage

The same balmy temperatures that make for pleasant picnicking can also cause improperly stored food to spoil. And if spoiled food is consumed, food poisoning can result. Keeping perishable foods lukewarm (60° to 140°F/16° to 60°C) or at room temperature allows rapid multiplication of the bacteria that can cause illness, even though the contaminated food may look and smell perfectly fresh.

For this reason, it's extremely important to observe the safety precautions outlined below, especially with foods particularly vulnerable to spoilage. These include, in general, foods that are high in protein or that contain eggs or dairy products—meats, poultry, fish and shellfish, custards, milk, cream, and mayonnaise, for example.

• Choose your picnic foods according to the weather and the distance you're traveling; avoid high-risk foods on long excursions or in very hot weather.

• Be meticulous about hygiene. When handling food, be sure your hands, utensils, and cutting surfaces are *clean;* always wash everything well with hot, soapy water after handling raw meat, poultry, or fish.

• Avoid preparing food far in advance, unless the recipe specifically permits it. The fresher the food, the less chance there is of bacterial growth.

• Don't keep foods at room temperature, either before the picnic or en route, if they're likely to spoil. Thaw frozen meat in the refrigerator, not on the kitchen counter; foods that are cooling after being cooked should sit only very briefly at room temperature; and all perishable foods should be carefully insulated when they're packed to travel, so they stay hot or cold (see page 90 for specific packing instructions).

• Cold foods must be thoroughly chilled and hot foods heated through *before* packing. Don't put foods into a cooler and expect to chill them on the way to the picnic; and never pack hot and cold foods together.

• Don't leave food that may spoil out on the picnic table while you play football or walk on the beach. Keep the food in the cooler or other insulated container until just before serving time, both to preserve freshness and to prevent contact with flies.

• Plan picnic quantities so you won't have leftovers—but if you do have food left, throw it away if it's susceptible to spoilage. *Even if it doesn't look or smell spoiled,* it has probably been kept out too long to be safe to eat.

... **Country-style Pâté (cont'd.)**

Place 1 of the bay leaves in a deep 1½ to 2-quart baking dish or terrine. Lay 3 of the bacon strips over bay leaf, extending bacon up sides of dish, if necessary. Pack meat mixture into dish. Arrange remaining bacon strips over top; garnish with remaining bay leaf.

Cover dish with foil, place it in a larger pan, and pour scalding water into larger pan to a depth of at least 1 inch. Bake in a 350° oven for about 2 hours or until juices run clear (cut a gash to test).

Uncover and let cool slightly. Lift out baking dish and place in another pan to catch any juices. Cover meat with a flat plate, slightly smaller than baking dish (or use heavy cardboard, cut to fit top of container and sealed in foil). Place a weight (such as a heavy can) on plate to press down surface of pâté. Refrigerate until next day.

Remove weight and plate; pour off and discard excess juices and fat. If made ahead, refrigerate for up to a week.

Transport in a cooler. To serve, cut into thick slices. Makes 8 to 10 servings.

Chicken Liver Pâté

(Pictured on page 42)

This flavorful pâté is not only quick to make, but silken smooth. If you like, add thinly sliced bits of black truffles for a French accent. Serve the pâté with crusty bread and *cornichons*.

½ cup (¼ lb.) butter or margarine
1 pound chicken livers, halved
¼ pound mushrooms, chopped
¼ cup chopped parsley
¼ cup chopped shallots or green onions (including tops)
½ teaspoon *each* thyme leaves and salt
2 tablespoons brandy or Madeira
½ cup dry red wine
1 cup (½ lb.) butter or margarine, cut into chunks
1 can (about ½ oz.) black truffles, thinly sliced or minced, or truffle trimmings (optional)
Lemon slices (optional)

In a wide frying pan over medium heat, melt the ½ cup butter. Add chicken livers, mushrooms, parsley, shallots, thyme, and salt. Cook, stirring often, until livers are browned on all sides but still slightly pink in center.

In a very small pan over low heat, warm brandy and set aflame (not beneath an exhaust fan or near flammable items). Pour over liver mixture and shake pan until flame dies. Add wine and heat to simmering. Remove from heat and let cool.

Whirl liver mixture in a blender or food processor. Add the 1 cup butter, blending until smooth. Stir in truffles and their liquid, if desired.

Pour into a deep, straight-sided oval or rectangular 4 to 5-cup pan or dish. Cover and refrigerate until firm, or for up to a week.

Garnish with lemon slices, if desired. Transport in a cooler. To serve, cut into slices and lift out pieces. Makes 12 to 16 servings.

Terrine of Pork, Veal & Ham

(Pictured on page 86)

In France, savory compact loaves of seasoned ground meat are called *terrines* after the straight-sided casseroles in which they're baked. Here's a classic terrine that features strips of veal and ham decoratively arranged between layers of ground meats.

6 strips bacon
¼ pound *each* boneless veal (cut from leg) and cooked ham, both meats cut ¼ inch thick
1 small onion, sliced
3 tablespoons brandy or apple juice
1¼ teaspoons thyme leaves
¾ teaspoon ground allspice
½ pound pork fat
1 pound *each* boneless veal stew meat and pork butt
4 parsley sprigs
2 eggs
⅓ cup half-and-half (light cream) or milk
2 teaspoons salt
¼ teaspoon pepper
2 bay leaves
6 black peppercorns

Place bacon in a wide frying pan and cover with water. Cover pan and simmer over low heat for 10 minutes. Drain bacon and pat dry. Set aside.

Cut the ¼ pound *each* veal and ham into strips ¼ inch wide. Place in a large bowl and add onions, brandy, and ¼ teaspoon *each* of the thyme and allspice. Mix and set aside.

To prepare with a food processor, cut pork fat and the 1 pound *each* veal and pork into 1-inch cubes. Using the metal blade, process, about a cup at a time, until finely chopped. Transfer to a large bowl. Remove onion from marinated meat mixture and process with parsley until finely chopped; add to chopped meats.

Drain liquid from marinated meat into processor and add eggs, half-and-half, remaining 1 teaspoon thyme and ½ teaspoon allspice, salt, and the ¼ teaspoon pepper. Process until blended. Combine with chopped meat mixture, and process, about a third at a time, until very finely ground and bits of pork fat are barely visible.

To prepare without a food processor, put pork fat, the 1 pound *each* veal and pork, onion (from the marinade), and parsley through a food chopper fitted with a fine blade. Turn into a bowl. Drain liquid from marinated meat into bowl, and add eggs, half-and-half, remaining 1 teaspoon thyme and ½ teaspoon allspice, salt, and the ¼ teaspoon pepper. Put through food chopper again.

Arrange 3 strips of the bacon lengthwise in a straight-sided 6-cup baking dish. Spread a third of the meat mixture in dish, and arrange half the marinated veal and ham strips lengthwise on top. Repeat, using another third of the meat mixture and remaining meat strips. Evenly spread remaining meat mixture in

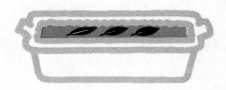

dish, and cover with remaining 3 strips bacon. Arrange bay leaves and peppercorns on top.

Cover tightly with foil, place in a larger pan, and pour scalding water into larger pan to a depth of at least 1 inch. Bake in a 350° oven for about 2 hours or until juices run clear (cut a gash to test).

Uncover and let cool slightly. Lift out baking dish and place in another pan to catch any juices. Cover meat with a flat plate, slightly smaller than baking dish (or use heavy cardboard, cut to fit top of container and sealed in foil). Place a weight (such as a heavy can) on plate to press down surface of terrine. Refrigerate until next day.

Just before transporting, lift off bay leaves and peppercorns, if desired. Immerse terrine in very hot water up to rim just until fat begins to melt (a few seconds); then turn out onto a serving board, and remove fat on outside. Slice, if desired. Return terrine (sliced or unsliced) to baking dish. Transport in a cooler. Makes 10 to 12 servings.

Boquitas

(Pictured on page 23)

Mound crisp little tortilla rounds with one or several different toppings to make the Guatemalan specialty called *boquitas*—"little mouthfuls." Eat them out of hand, or offer plates and forks for those guests who want to pile their boquitas high.

Though usually considered an appetizer, boquitas can easily become a whole meal, accompanied by beer or cider, fresh fruit, and cookies for dessert.

Shredded Pork (recipe follows)

Fresh Tomato Salsa (recipe follows)

Cabbage & Carrot Slaw (page 30)

Simmered Black Beans (page 38)

18 to 24 **corn tortillas**

Salad oil

Salt (optional)

1 pint **potato or macaroni salad,** purchased or homemade

1 large package (8 oz.) **cream cheese**

½ pound **jack cheese,** shredded

1 cup finely chopped or thinly sliced **radishes**

1 or 2 cans (1 lb. *each*) sliced pickled **beets,** drained

1½ to 2 cups **guacamole** or avocado dip, purchased or homemade

2 or 3 **limes,** cut into wedges

Prepare Shredded Pork, Fresh Tomato Salsa, Cabbage & Carrot Slaw, and Simmered Black Beans. Refrigerate until next day.

With a 2-inch cooky cutter, cut each tortilla into 5 smaller ones. Pour oil into a wide frying pan to a depth of about ¼ inch. Heat oil over medium-high heat and cook tortillas, 6 to 8 at a time, until crisp and lightly browned on both sides; lift out and drain. Salt lightly, if desired. Let cool and pack in a container.

Reheat the pork and the black beans, and transport as directed on page 90. Pack salsa, slaw, potato salad, cheeses, radishes, beets, guacamole, and limes in separate containers, and transport in a cooler.

To serve, set out tortilla rounds and containers of toppings to be mounded on top. Makes 6 servings.

Shredded Pork. Place a 3-pound **pork shoulder** in a 5-quart kettle; add just enough **water** to cover meat. Add 1 large **onion,** chopped; ½ tea-

spoon *each* **oregano leaves** and **cumin seeds;** and 8 **black peppercorns.** Cover and simmer over low heat until fork-tender (2 to 2½ hours).

Lift out meat (reserve stock and set aside), drain, and place in a roasting pan. Bake, uncovered, in a 350° oven for 45 minutes or until well browned.

Let cool; then shred meat, discarding fat and bone. (At this point, you may cover and refrigerate for up to 2 days.)

Just before transporting, place meat in a 3 to 4-quart pan, and drizzle with ¼ to ½ cup reserved **stock** or water; cover and cook over medium heat, stirring often, until heated through. Transport as directed on page 90. Makes about 5 cups.

Fresh Tomato Salsa. In a large bowl, combine 1 cup peeled, seeded, and chopped **tomatoes;** ¼ cup finely chopped **onion;** 3 tablespoons chopped **fresh mint** or crumbled dry mint; 2 teaspoons chopped **fresh coriander** (cilantro); and ⅛ teaspoon **crushed red pepper.** Season to taste with **salt.** If made ahead, cover and refrigerate until next day.

With a slotted spoon, transfer tomato mixture to a container and cover. Makes about 1 cup.

Carrot Soup

(Pictured on page 67)

Offer brightly colored carrot soup hot or cold, depending on your menu and your destination. If you serve it with croutons, you'll need to take along spoons; by itself, the soup is smooth enough to sip from a mug.

(Continued on page 25)

Guatemalan Appetizer Party

Boquitas (page 22), traditional Guatemalan appetizers whose name means "little mouthfuls," quickly become big mouthfuls, thanks to the bountiful array of colorful and tasty toppings you stack on crisp little tortilla rounds. From cool Cabbage & Carrot Slaw (page 30), fresh tomato salsa, and shredded cheese to hot shredded pork and Simmered Black Beans (page 38), the possible combinations are practically unlimited. For appropriate accompaniments to this feast, offer delicate Guatemalan Sugar Cookies (page 73) and Latin American beer.

The Cheese Board

It's no wonder that cheeses are so often a mainstay of picnic meals. They're simple, nourishing, easy to eat, full of interesting flavors and textures, and at their best when served at room temperature—all of which makes them ideal for enjoyment on an outdoor excursion.

Making your selection. Countless varieties of cheese are available, and quality varies, so find a reputable cheese merchant who can answer questions and help guide your selection. Ask to taste before you buy, unless you're purchasing prewrapped cheeses.

Firm and semisoft cheeses can be purchased ahead of time, but buy soft cheeses and goat cheeses (*chèvres*) only a few days in advance; tell the cheese merchant when you plan to serve them so you'll be sure to receive cheeses at the appropriate stage of ripeness.

Unless they come wrapped airtight, package cheeses in plastic wrap. Don't use foil; the acid in cheese may react with it. Store them in the refrigerator.

Fresh cheeses are mild, rich, and creamy unripened cheeses with no rind. Some are flavored with herbs or pepper. Examples are Saint-André, boursault, boursin, and Gervais.

Soft cheeses have thin rinds and smooth, buttery interiors that are often spreadable at room temperature. Their flavors range from mild and delicate to highly aromatic and pungent. Try Brie, Camembert, Revidoux, Pont l'Evêque, Coulommiers, carré de l'est, and Livarot.

Semisoft cheeses are firmer than soft cheeses, but still smooth and rich in texture. They may be coated with wax or have natural rinds; flavors are mild to pronounced. Choices include Havarti, Port Salut, Monterey jack, Münster, Saint-Paulin, and Bel Paese.

Chèvres, French goat cheeses, have many distinctive shapes. Some are coated with vegetable ash; others are wrapped in leaves or sprinkled with pepper or herbs. All are tart and zingy in flavor. Some commonly available types are Sainte-Maure, pyramide, banon, and Saint-Marcellin.

Blue-veined cheeses range from creamy to crumbly in texture; marbled with blue green veins, they're tangy and assertive in flavor. Stilton, Roquefort, and Gorgonzola are some popular varieties.

Firm cheeses are dense, though sometimes quite supple; some have holes. Flavors can be mellow and nutty or sharp. Try lappi, Edam, sharp Cheddar, Gruyère, Jarlsberg, and Emmenthaler.

Processed cheeses are generally blends of two or more cheeses, heated and emulsified so they have smooth textures and keep well. Many types are available; some are embellished with herbs, nuts, fruits, seeds, or pepper.

Taking cheeses to the picnic. Carry your cheeses wrapped in plastic wrap to keep them fresh and to help softer cheeses hold their shape. Cheeses from the refrigerator take from 30 minutes to 3 hours to come to room temperature, depending on their size, the temperature outside, and the way they're transported. If it's a hot day or if you won't be serving the cheeses for several hours, you may want to put them in a cooler so they don't sweat and get messy; otherwise, just carry them in a basket.

Serving suggestions. Take along knives (butter knives will do), and a cheese slicer if you want thin slices of firmer cheeses. Offer crusty bread or plain crackers (and sweet butter, if you like); pâtés and delicatessen meats alongside can turn your cheese board into a main course. When the cheeses are for dessert, try pairing them with fruits. And if you're serving wine, keep in mind that light, dry wines are best with subtly flavored cheeses; stronger, more pungent cheeses require more robust, fuller-bodied wines.

... Carrot Soup (cont'd.)

2 pounds bony chicken pieces (backs, wings, and necks)
3 or 4 parsley sprigs
5 or 6 carrots
1 large onion, sliced
¾ teaspoon salt
4 cups water
Jumbo Croutons (optional—recipe follows)
½ cup heavy cream
¾ teaspoon thyme leaves
Salt and white pepper
Chopped parsley

Tie chicken pieces and parsley sprigs in a bag made from a single thickness of cheesecloth. Place in a large kettle. Add carrots, onion, the ¾ teaspoon salt, and water. Bring to a boil over high heat. Cover, reduce heat, and simmer for 2 hours.

Meanwhile, prepare Jumbo Croutons, if desired, and store in an airtight container.

Let broth cool slightly; then lift out bag and drain well. Discard bones and parsley sprigs.

Remove carrots, onion, and some of the broth from kettle, and whirl in a blender or food processor until smooth. Return vegetable purée to broth in pan, and stir in cream and thyme. Season to taste with salt and pepper. Cover loosely with foil; refrigerate until next day.

To serve hot, reheat soup to simmering and transport in a preheated thermos (see page 90). To serve cold, season again with salt and pepper, if desired; transport soup in a prechilled thermos (see page 90).

Sprinkle each serving with chopped parsley. Pass croutons, if desired. Makes about 6 cups.

Jumbo Croutons. Cut day-old **French bread** (about a third of a 1-lb. loaf) into 1-inch cubes to make 2 cups total; evenly spread cubes on a rimmed baking sheet. Bake in a 300° oven for 10 minutes. Remove from oven and set aside; reduce

oven temperature to 275°.

In a wide frying pan over medium heat, melt 4 tablespoons **butter** or margarine. Stir in 1 large clove **garlic,** minced or pressed, and 1 teaspoon **parsley flakes.** Remove from heat. Add toasted bread cubes and stir to coat evenly.

Spread cubes on baking sheet and bake in a 275° oven for 15 minutes or until crisp and lightly browned. Let cool completely. Makes about 2 cups croutons.

Cucumber Cream Soup

This refreshing soup is a snap to make—there's no cooking required.

3 medium-size cucumbers, peeled and cut into cubes
1 clove garlic, halved
3 tablespoons *each* chopped parsley and chopped onion
1 cup regular-strength chicken broth
3 tablespoons white wine vinegar
1 pint (2 cups) plain yogurt
½ pint (1 cup) sour cream
Salt and pepper
Chopped fresh mint (optional)
Shelled sunflower seeds (optional)

In a blender or food processor, combine cucumbers, garlic, parsley, onion, broth, and vinegar; whirl until well blended. Pour about half the mixture into a container; set aside.

Add 1 cup of the yogurt and ½ cup of the sour cream to cucumber mixture in blender; whirl until smooth. Transfer to a large bowl. Pour reserved cucumber mixture into blender container, and add remaining yogurt and sour cream. Whirl until smooth. Add to bowl and season to taste with salt and

pepper. Cover and refrigerate until well chilled.

Stir soup well; season again with salt and pepper, if desired. Transport in a prechilled thermos (see page 90). Garnish servings with mint and sunflower seeds, if desired. Makes about 1½ quarts.

Cold Berry Soup

Serve fruit soup as an opener at a picnic brunch, or with butter cookies as dessert after lunch or dinner.

2 cups water
3 tablespoons quick-cooking tapioca
½ cup sugar
¼ teaspoon salt
1 whole cinnamon stick
1 teaspoon grated lemon peel
⅓ cup lemon juice
1½ cups (about 8 oz.) frozen unsweetened blueberries
1 jar (14 oz.) lingonberries
Sour cream

In a 3 to 4-quart pan, combine water, tapioca, sugar, salt, cinnamon, lemon peel, lemon juice, and blueberries. Bring to a boil over medium-high heat, stirring constantly; reduce heat and simmer, stirring occasionally, for 5 minutes. Remove from heat and stir in lingonberries and their liquid until blended. Cover loosely with foil and refrigerate until well chilled.

(Continued on page 27)

Fireside Supper

When it's bitter cold outside, you can devise a cozy indoor picnic in front of a crackling fire. Warming menu ideas are mugs of Creamy Herbed Walnut Soup (page 27); Empanadas (page 44) filled with a robust meat, vegetable, and raisin mixture; and zesty Avocado Vegetable Dip (page 17) with red pepper strips, cucumber wedges, and tortilla chips.

. . . Cold Berry Soup (cont'd.)

Remove and discard cinnamon stick; transport soup in a prechilled thermos (see page 90). Pack sour cream in a cooler. To serve, pour soup into small bowls and pass sour cream to spoon over each serving. Makes about 5 cups.

Creamy Herbed Walnut Soup

(Pictured on page 26)

Here's a rich, creamy soup that will please vegetarians—and everyone else, too. The nuts are puréed, so the soup can be sipped; you don't need to take spoons.

1½ cups chopped walnuts
2 cups milk
½ bay leaf
¼ teaspoon *each* thyme leaves and dry basil
2 tablespoons chopped parsley
2 tablespoons butter or margarine
1 medium-size onion, sliced
½ cup thinly sliced celery
2 tablespoons all-purpose flour
3 cups regular-strength chicken broth
2 tablespoons dry sherry
Salt and pepper
Finely chopped chives or green onions (optional)

Place walnuts in a pan, cover with water, and bring to a boil over high heat; boil for 3 minutes; then drain. Return nuts to pan and add milk, bay leaf, thyme, basil, and parsley. Heat to scalding; then cover and set aside for 20 minutes.

Meanwhile, in a 3-quart pan over medium heat, melt butter. Add onion and celery and cook for about 5 minutes. Stir in flour and cook until bubbly. Gradually stir in broth; cook, stirring, until soup comes

to a boil. Reduce heat and simmer gently for 10 minutes.

Remove bay leaf and add milk mixture to soup. In a blender or food processor, whirl soup, a small amount at a time, until smooth. (At this point, you may cover and refrigerate until next day.)

Just before transporting, reheat to simmering. Add sherry, and season to taste with salt and pepper. Transport in a preheated thermos (see page 90). To serve, pour into mugs or cups and garnish each serving with chives, if desired. Makes about 1½ quarts.

Clam & Corn Chowder

Two traditional chowders combine to create this thick, creamy soup that's also fast and easy to make.

2 tablespoons butter or margarine
1 small onion, chopped
2 cans (6½ oz. *each*) chopped clams
1 bottle (8 oz.) clam juice
1 can (17 oz.) cream-style corn
1 cup milk
¼ teaspoon liquid hot pepper seasoning
8 strips bacon, crisply cooked, drained, and crumbled (optional)

In a 3½ or 4-quart pan over medium heat, melt butter. Add onion and cook until limp. Stir in clams and their liquid, clam juice, corn, milk, and hot pepper seasoning; cook, stirring occasionally, until heated through (about 10 minutes).

Transport in a preheated thermos (see page 90). To serve, pour into small bowls and sprinkle each serving with crumbled bacon, if desired. Makes about 7 cups.

Alphabet Vegetable Soup

(Pictured on page 18)

Alphabet soup is always a hit with children, especially when it's filled with chunks of fresh vegetables, as well as pasta. For more sophisticated picnickers, you can substitute any other type of small soup macaroni.

3 tablespoons butter or margarine
1 large onion, chopped
1 cup *each* peeled and diced carrots and red thin-skinned potato
½ cup diced celery
1 can (about 1 lb.) tomatoes
2 beef bouillon cubes dissolved in 3½ cups water
½ teaspoon dry basil
Salt and pepper
3 tablespoons alphabet macaroni
Boiling salted water

In a 5-quart Dutch oven over medium heat, melt butter. Add onion and cook until limp. Stir in carrots, potato, celery, tomatoes (break up with a spoon) and their liquid, bouillon, and basil. Bring to a boil over high heat. Cover, reduce heat, and simmer until vegetables are tender when pierced (30 to 35 minutes). Season to taste with salt and pepper.

Meanwhile, cook macaroni in boiling salted water for 5 minutes or until tender. Drain, rinse under cold water, and drain again. Add macaroni to soup. If made ahead, let cool slightly, cover loosely, and refrigerate until next day. Just before transporting, reheat soup to simmering.

Transport in a preheated wide-mouthed thermos (see page 90). Makes about 1½ quarts.

Salads & Side Dishes

All the trimmings: old favorites and new inspirations

For color and crunch, variety and sparkle, choose salads and side dishes that not only complement your entrée but also are exciting creations in their own right. Select a side dish to help you carry out an ethnic theme, or to take advantage of seasonal produce; or choose one that adds a contrasting taste or texture to your main dish.

In this chapter, we offer ideas for all of the above, with an accent on originality. Potato salad gets a bright

green dressing in one recipe, peanuts and bacon in another. Deviled eggs are included, with four unusual variations. Rice, pasta, and autumn fruits appear as salad components; the flavors of Mexico, Italy, and the south of France are featured in other dishes.

Most of the recipes can be made well in advance and refrigerated until you're ready to leave home. Some must be carried in insulated containers, but others can just travel in a picnic basket.

Garden Vegetable Salad Bowl

(Pictured on page 39)

A vivid mélange of lightly cooked vegetables marinates in a lemony dressing. This salad makes good use of the summer's bountiful harvest.

Salt
1½ cups bite-size cauliflowerets
1½ cups thinly sliced carrots
1½ cups thinly sliced crookneck squash
1 medium-size red or green bell pepper, seeded and cut into thin strips
⅓ cup thinly sliced green onions (including tops)
1½ cups green beans, cut into 1-inch pieces
1½ cups bite-size broccoli flowerets
Oil-Lemon Dressing (recipe follows)

Pour water into a wide frying pan to a depth of about 1 inch. Add salt and bring to a boil. Add cauliflower and cook, uncovered, over medium-high heat just until tender when pierced (3 to 4 minutes). With a slotted spoon, transfer cauliflower to a salad bowl.

Add carrots to cooking water and cook, uncovered, just until tender when pierced (4 to 5 minutes). With a slotted spoon, add carrots to salad bowl.

Place squash in cooking water and cook, uncovered, for 3 minutes (add more boiling water, if necessary). With a slotted spoon, lift out squash and add to salad bowl. Stir in pepper and onions.

Add green beans and broccoli to cooking water and cook, uncovered, just until tender when pierced (about 5 minutes). Drain well and set aside.

Prepare Oil-Lemon Dressing and pour over squash mixture; stir gently to coat vegetables. Place green beans and broccoli on top. Cover and refrigerate for at least 4 hours or until next day.

About 30 minutes before serving, stir beans and broccoli into salad. Makes 6 to 8 servings.

Oil-Lemon Dressing. In a small bowl, stir together ⅔ cup **salad oil;** ¼ teaspoon grated **lemon peel;** ⅓ cup **lemon juice;** ½ teaspoon *each* **salt, sugar, dry basil,** and **prepared mustard;** and ¼ teaspoon **pepper.**

Green Pea & Cottage Cheese Salad

Briefly cooked and quickly chilled, fresh peas make colorful and delicious salads. If fresh peas aren't available, substitute frozen ones.

6 to 8 green onions
2 pounds peas, shelled, or 1 package (10 oz.) frozen peas
1 small green pepper, seeded and diced
1 pint (2 cups) small curd cottage cheese
½ teaspoon salt
⅛ teaspoon pepper
½ teaspoon curry powder or 1 teaspoon dill weed
2 tablespoons finely chopped parsley

Slice white parts of green onions; set green tops aside. In a small pan over medium heat, cook peas and onion slices in boiling water to cover, just until tender (about 8 minutes for fresh peas, 5 minutes for frozen peas). Drain, rinse under cold water, and drain again.

Slice green onion tops and place in a bowl; stir in green

pepper, cottage cheese, salt, pepper, curry, parsley, and peas. Cover and refrigerate for about 3 hours. Transport in a cooler. Makes 4 to 6 servings.

Mushroom - Artichoke Salad

(Pictured on page 91)

Cherry tomatoes add a bright, juicy accent to the marinated vegetables in this salad.

2 packages (9 oz. *each*) frozen artichoke hearts
1 pound mushrooms, sliced
½ cup olive oil or salad oil
2 tablespoons *each* lemon juice and white wine vinegar
1 clove garlic, minced or pressed
¾ teaspoon salt
¼ teaspoon pepper
½ teaspoon *each* oregano and thyme leaves
1 bay leaf
2 cups cherry tomatoes

Cook artichoke hearts according to package directions; drain and let cool.

In a bowl, combine artichokes and mushrooms.

In a small bowl, stir together oil, lemon juice, vinegar, garlic, salt, pepper, oregano, thyme, and bay leaf. Pour over vegetables; mix well. Cover and refrigerate for at least 4 hours or until next day.

Just before transporting, remove bay leaf; cut tomatoes in half and stir into salad. Makes 8 servings.

Cabbage & Carrot Slaw

(Pictured on page 23)

Mellow, sweet-tart slaw complements a variety of picnic foods. Offer it as part of the Guatemalan appetizer party (page 5), mound it on grilled frankfurters or sausages, or serve it as a side dish with cold cooked ham, smoked tongue, or barbecued beef.

- **2 cups finely shredded cabbage**
- **1 cup shredded carrots**
- **¼ cup thinly sliced green onions (including tops)**
- **⅓ cup white wine vinegar**
- **3 tablespoons sugar**
- **¼ teaspoon garlic salt**
- **⅛ teaspoon *each* pepper, ground cumin, oregano leaves, and dry mustard**

In a 1½ to 2-quart container with a lid, combine cabbage, carrots, and onions.

In a small bowl, stir together vinegar, sugar, garlic salt, pepper, cumin, oregano, and mustard until sugar is dissolved; pour over vegetables and mix well. Cover and refrigerate for at least 4 hours or until next day. Mix well before serving. Makes about 3 cups or 4 to 6 side-dish servings.

Mixed Bean & Artichoke Salad

(Pictured on page 34)

A superb dressing—one that includes capers and the marinade from artichoke hearts—elevates this sturdy combination to regal status. If you like, garnish with slices of hard-cooked egg.

- **2 cans (15 oz. *each*) red kidney beans, drained**
- **1 can (6 oz.) pitted ripe olives, drained**
- **1 can (1 lb.) dilled green beans or cut green beans, drained**
- **1 jar (4 oz.) sliced pimentos, drained**
- **1 can (8 oz.) garbanzos, drained**
- **1 jar (6 oz.) marinated artichoke hearts**
- **1½ cups *each* thinly sliced celery and thinly sliced carrots**
- **2 large dill pickles, thinly sliced**
- **1 large mild red onion, thinly sliced**
  Oil & Vinegar Dressing (recipe follows)
- **2 hard-cooked eggs, sliced (optional)**

In a container with a lid, combine kidney beans, olives, green beans, pimentos, and garbanzos. Drain artichokes, reserving marinade for dressing. Cut artichokes in half. Setting a few aside for garnish, add remaining artichokes to bean mixture along with celery, carrots, pickles, and onion.

Prepare Oil & Vinegar Dressing and pour over bean mixture; stir well. Cover and refrigerate until next day; stir several times.

To serve, stir salad well. Arrange egg slices, if desired, and reserved artichokes on top. Makes 8 to 10 servings.

Oil & Vinegar Dressing. Measure reserved artichoke marinade in a 1-quart glass measure and add enough **olive oil** or salad oil to make ¾ cup *total.* Add ¾ cup **white wine vinegar;** 2 tablespoons **chopped parsley;** 3 large cloves **garlic,** minced or pressed; 2 tablespoons **lemon juice;** 1 tablespoon *each* **dry basil** and **ground coriander;** 3 tablespoons **capers,** drained and chopped; and **salt** and **pepper** to taste. Stir until well blended.

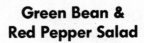

Green Bean & Red Pepper Salad

(Pictured on page 31)

To help retain their fresh green hue, cook the beans very lightly; then chill and toss with the marinated pepper strips just before serving. You'll be rewarded with a cheery-looking salad in bright garden colors.

- **1 pound small green beans**
  Basil-Mustard Dressing (recipe follows)
- **1 medium-size red bell pepper, seeded and cut into slivers**
  Red leaf lettuce

Cut and discard ends from beans; leave beans whole. Pour water into a 3-quart pan to a depth of about 2 inches. Bring to a boil; add beans. Cook, uncovered, just until tender-crisp (about 5 minutes). Drain, rinse under cold water, and drain again. Place in a bowl, cover, and refrigerate.

Prepare Basil-Mustard Dressing. In a large container with a lid, combine red pepper slivers with dressing; cover and refrigerate. Transport beans and pepper mixture separately in a cooler. To serve, add beans to pepper mixture; stir gently until beans are thoroughly coated with dressing. With a slotted spoon, lift out vegetables and serve on lettuce leaves. Makes 4 to 6 servings.

Basil-Mustard Dressing. In a small bowl, combine 3 tablespoons **red wine vinegar;** 1 tablespoon **Dijon mustard;** 1 clove **garlic,** minced or pressed; and ½ teaspoon *each* **sugar, salt,** and **dry basil.** Using a fork or wire whip, gradually beat in ⅓ cup **olive oil** or salad oil until well blended.

Provençal Picnic

Bright colors and bold flavors characterize this *pique-nique* from the sunny region of Provence in southern France. Anchovies and Niçoise olives embellish the tops of garlicky Tomato Tarts Niçoise (page 59); they're firm enough to be eaten out of hand. Crunchy Green Bean & Red Pepper Salad (page 30) and baguettes with a variety of French cheeses are perfect foils for the tomato tarts. But don't stop there—complete the meal with wine, fruit, and rich, apricot-glazed Pine Nut Tarts (page 82).

Chile-spiced Bean Salad

(Pictured on page 91)

Bits of chile mingle with corn and three kinds of beans in this colorful salad that stays crisp for hours.

> Spicy Dressing (recipe follows)
> 1 can (about 1 lb.) *each* red kidney beans, pinto beans, and garbanzos
> 1 can (1 lb.) whole kernel corn
> 1 large stalk celery, thinly sliced
> 5 green onions (including tops), thinly sliced
> ¼ cup chopped parsley
> 1 can (4 oz.) diced green chiles

Prepare Spicy Dressing and set aside.

Drain kidney beans, pinto beans, and garbanzos; rinse under cold water and drain again. Turn into a container with a lid. Drain corn; add to bean mixture along with celery, onions, parsley, and chiles.

Pour dressing over vegetables and mix well. Cover and refrigerate for 6 hours or until next day. Makes 8 to 10 servings.

Spicy Dressing. In a 2-cup glass measure, stir together ¾ cup **salad oil**; ¼ cup **wine vinegar**; 1 clove **garlic**, minced or pressed; ¾ teaspoon **salt**; 1 teaspoon *each* **chili powder** and **oregano leaves**; ¼ teaspoon **ground cumin**; and a dash of **pepper.**

Peanut Potato Salad

Salted peanuts and crisp vegetables give this salad appealing flavor and crunch.

> 2 pounds red thin-skinned potatoes
> ½ cup *each* chopped green pepper and chopped celery
> ¾ cup thinly sliced green onions (including tops)
> ¼ cup *each* chopped parsley and diced cucumber
> ¾ cup salted Spanish peanuts
> 6 strips bacon, crisply cooked, drained, and crumbled
> ½ cup mayonnaise
> 2 tablespoons cider vinegar
> 1 tablespoon crunchy peanut butter
> 1 teaspoon curry powder (optional)
> Salt and pepper

Pour water into a 3 to 4-quart pan to a depth of 1 inch. Bring to a boil over high heat; add potatoes. Cover, reduce heat, and cook just until tender when pierced (20 to 30 minutes). Drain and let cool. Peel, if desired, and cut into ½-inch cubes. In a bowl, combine potatoes, green pepper, celery, green onions, parsley, cucumber, ½ cup of the nuts, and bacon; mix well.

In a small bowl, stir together mayonnaise, vinegar, peanut butter, and curry powder, if desired. Pour over potato mixture and stir well. Season to taste with salt and pepper. Cover and refrigerate for at least 4 hours or until next day. Transport in a cooler.

Just before serving, stir well and garnish with remaining ¼ cup nuts. Makes about 6 servings.

Parsley Potato Salad

(Pictured on page 91)

For a new twist on the traditional potato salad, try this light, fresh-tasting version that combines sliced potatoes with a bright green oil and vinegar dressing.

> 2 pounds small red thin-skinned potatoes
> 1 large stalk celery, finely chopped
> 1 hard-cooked egg
> 1 small clove garlic, minced or pressed
> 4 canned anchovy fillets
> 2 tablespoons Dijon mustard
> ½ teaspoon sugar
> ¼ teaspoon liquid hot pepper seasoning
> ⅓ cup olive oil or salad oil
> 3 tablespoons white wine vinegar
> Salt and pepper
> 3 green onions (including tops), finely chopped
> ½ cup chopped parsley

Pour water into a 3 to 4-quart pan to a depth of 1 inch. Bring to a boil over high heat; add potatoes. Cover, reduce heat, and cook just until tender when pierced (20 to 30 minutes). Drain and let cool. Peel, if desired, and thinly slice into a bowl. Add celery.

In a blender or food processor, whirl egg, garlic, anchovies, mustard, sugar, hot pepper seasoning, oil, and vinegar until smooth. Season to taste with salt and pepper; then stir in onions and parsley.

Pour dressing over potato mixture and stir gently. Cover and refrigerate for at least 4 hours or until next day. Transport in a cooler. Makes 6 to 8 servings.

Sweet Potato Salad

Crisp vegetables and fruit complement the mellow sweetness of this golden potato salad. It's a good candidate for an outdoor holiday feast with hot or cold cooked turkey or ham.

1 to 1½ pounds sweet potatoes
1 cup thinly sliced celery
½ cup thinly sliced green onions (including tops)
1 large red-skinned apple, cored and diced
½ cup mayonnaise
1 teaspoon prepared mustard
½ teaspoon grated orange peel
1 tablespoon orange juice
2 tablespoons finely chopped crystallized ginger
   Salt and pepper
   Crisp greens (optional)

Place potatoes in a 3 to 4-quart pan. Cover with water and bring to a boil over high heat. Cover, reduce heat, and cook until tender when pierced (about 30 minutes); drain. When cool enough to handle, peel potatoes and cut into ½-inch cubes. In a bowl, combine potatoes, celery, onions, and apple.

In a small bowl, stir together mayonnaise, mustard, orange peel, orange juice, and ginger. Pour over potato mixture and stir well. Season to taste with salt and pepper. Cover and refrigerate for at least 2 hours or until next day. Transport in a cooler.

To serve, tuck crisp greens around salad, if desired. Makes 4 to 6 servings.

Sweet & Tart Rice Salad

Bits of crunchy vegetables mingle with cooked rice in this cool salad that makes a fine accompaniment to barbecued meats. For extra flavor, you can add a garnish of small cooked shrimp.

2 cups cold cooked white or brown rice
½ cup *each* chopped carrot, green onions (including tops), and cucumber
¼ cup white wine vinegar
2 tablespoons sugar
½ teaspoon salt
¼ pound small cooked shrimp (optional)
   Butter lettuce leaves
2 tablespoons toasted sesame seeds

In a salad bowl, combine rice, carrot, green onions, and cucumber. In a 1-cup glass measure, stir together vinegar, sugar, and salt; stir into rice mixture. Cover and refrigerate for at least 1 hour or until next day. Transport salad and shrimp in a cooler.

Just before serving, stir salad well, tuck lettuce around salad, and sprinkle with sesame seeds. Garnish with shrimp, if desired. Makes 6 servings.

Chunky Taco Salad

Inspired by the flavorful ingredients of a Mexican taco, this fresh-tasting, crunchy salad goes well with barbecued steak or hamburgers, fried chicken, or cold cooked beef or turkey.

1 small head iceberg lettuce
¼ cup thinly sliced green onions (including tops)
1 can (15 oz.) red kidney beans, drained
1 can (2¼ oz.) sliced ripe olives, drained
½ cup sharp Cheddar cheese, cut into julienne strips
2 cups coarsely crushed tortilla chips or corn chips
   Salsa Dressing (recipe follows)
1 medium-size firm ripe avocado
1 large tomato, cut into wedges
   Fresh coriander (cilantro) sprigs (optional)

Cut lettuce into ¾-inch chunks. Place in a large salad bowl. Top with onions, beans, olives, and cheese. Sprinkle chips over top; *do not mix.* Cover and refrigerate for about 3 hours.

Prepare Salsa Dressing.

Just before serving, pour dressing over salad mixture and stir well. Peel, pit, and slice avocado; distribute over salad along with tomato and coriander, if desired. Makes 4 to 6 servings.

Salsa Dressing. In a small container with a lid, stir together ⅓ cup **salad oil,** 3 tablespoons **red wine vinegar,** 1 teaspoon **chili powder,** ¼ teaspoon *each* **garlic salt** and **ground cumin,** and ⅛ teaspoon **crushed red pepper.** Stir in 1 can (7 oz.) **green chile salsa;** mix well.

Pasta & Pepper Salad

For an Italian-style *alfresco* feast, offer a salad of shell macaroni dressed with oil and vinegar and spiked with basil and Parmesan cheese.

8 ounces small shell macaroni
½ cup olive oil or salad oil
⅓ cup white wine vinegar
1 tablespoon dry basil
1 clove garlic, minced or pressed
⅓ cup grated Parmesan cheese
   Salt and pepper
2 tablespoons chopped parsley
1 large red or green bell pepper, seeded and diced

Cook macaroni according to package directions. Drain, rinse under cold water, and drain again.

In a salad bowl, stir together oil, vinegar, basil, garlic, and Parmesan cheese.

(Continued on page 35)

Beach Barbecue

After a long afternoon of building sand castles and splashing in the surf, settle down to a summery barbecue of grilled hamburgers on French rolls, tender Barbecued Corn on the Cob (page 35), Mixed Bean & Artichoke Salad (page 30), and Crunchy Egg Dip (page 17) with potato chips. At dessert time, Honey-Applesauce Cupcakes (page 77) play a sweet counterpoint to salty sea air.

... Pasta & Pepper Salad (cont'd.)

Mix in macaroni and season to taste with salt and pepper. Cover and refrigerate for at least 4 hours or until next day.

Just before serving, stir in parsley and red pepper. Makes 4 to 6 servings.

Macaroni Salad

When you need a portable salad to feed a crowd, consider this perennial picnic favorite. It's perfect with cold cuts, ham loaf, or grilled sausages—and it serves a hungry dozen.

 1 pound salad macaroni
12 large green onions (including tops), sliced
 4 hard-cooked eggs, chopped
 1 cup thinly sliced celery
12 strips bacon, crisply cooked, drained, and crumbled
 1 jar (4 oz.) sliced pimentos, drained
 1 cup chopped dill pickles
1½ cups mayonnaise
 1 tablespoon prepared horseradish
 2 teaspoons prepared mustard
 1 tablespoon dill pickle juice (optional)
   Salt and pepper

Cook macaroni according to package directions. Drain, rinse under cold water, and drain again. Turn macaroni into a large bowl; add onions (reserving some green tops for garnish), eggs, celery, bacon, pimentos, and pickles.

In a small bowl, stir together mayonnaise, horseradish, mustard, and pickle juice, if desired. Stir into macaroni mixture. Season to taste with salt and pepper; garnish with reserved onion tops. Cover and refrigerate for at least 4 hours or until next day. Transport in a cooler. Makes 12 to 14 servings.

Harvest Fruit Salad

Autumn fruits, lightly dressed and topped with nuts, go well with turkey, ham, chicken, or pork.

 2 large oranges
 1 cup diced celery
 1 cup halved and seeded grapes
 ½ cup quartered pitted dates or whole raisins
 ⅓ cup mayonnaise
 ½ teaspoon prepared mustard
 ¼ teaspoon celery salt
 5 large red-skinned apples or firm ripe pears, unpeeled
 2 large bananas
 ½ cup coarsely chopped walnuts

Cut peel and white membrane from oranges. Holding oranges over a bowl to catch juice, lift out sections; reserve 3 tablespoons of the juice.

In a large bowl, combine orange sections, celery, grapes, and dates; cover and refrigerate until next day. In a small bowl, stir together mayonnaise, mustard, and celery salt; cover and refrigerate until next day.

About 1 hour before serving, cut apples into large cubes and bananas into ¼-inch diagonal slices; add reserved orange juice and stir gently until fruit is completely coated. Add to date mixture and top with dressing; stir gently. Cover and transport in a cooler.

Just before serving, sprinkle with nuts. Makes about 10 servings.

Brussels Sprouts in Mustard-Herb Dressing

None of the crispness or fresh color of this salad is lost as it stands. To make serving easier, tuck a slotted spoon in with the rest of your picnic gear before you leave home.

1¼ pounds Brussels sprouts
   Lightly salted water
 1 teaspoon *each* prepared mustard, Worcestershire, sugar, and salt
 ½ teaspoon dry basil
 ¼ teaspoon *each* thyme leaves and pepper
 ¼ cup red wine vinegar
 1 cup salad oil
 2 cups cherry tomatoes, cut in half
 ½ cup thinly sliced green onions (including tops)

Trim and discard stem ends from sprouts, then slice each sprout in half lengthwise. In a 3 to 4-quart pan over high heat, bring a large quantity of lightly salted water to a boil. Add sprouts; reduce heat and simmer, uncovered, just until tender-crisp (about 7 minutes). Immediately turn into a colander and drain thoroughly.

In a small bowl, stir together mustard, Worcestershire, sugar, salt, basil, thyme, pepper, vinegar, and oil.

Transfer warm Brussels sprouts to a container with a lid; pour mustard dressing over sprouts and stir to coat evenly. Cover and refrigerate for at least 4 hours or until next day.

Just before serving, stir in cherry tomatoes and onions. Makes 4 to 6 servings.

Barbecued Corn on the Cob

(Pictured on page 34)

Two of summer's most appealing joys—barbecuing and corn on the cob—are combined in this easy-to-prepare picnic

... Barbecued Corn (cont'd.)

vegetable. It's a perfect accompaniment to barbecued meats or poultry, and it goes right on the grill with them.

> **4 ears corn on the cob, unhusked**
> **Butter or margarine**
> **Salt and pepper**

Pull husks back from ears of corn, leaving husks attached at base, and remove silk. Cut off 2 or 3 pieces of husk; cut lengthwise into ½-inch strips and set aside. Replace husks and tie each ear closed with 1 or 2 of the reserved strips to seal completely. Soak in ice water for about 30 minutes. Drain well; seal in plastic bags and transport in a cooler.

Place corn on a grill 4 to 6 inches above a solid bed of glowing coals. Cook for 15 to 20 minutes, turning occasionally to cook evenly. To serve, discard husks and season corn with butter, salt, and pepper. Makes 4 servings.

Ratatouille

(Pictured on page 78)

You can transport this popular Mediterranean vegetable stew in your picnic basket. To allow vegetable flavors ample time to mellow, prepare the dish at least a day ahead. It's best served at room temperature.

> **2 medium-size eggplants (about 1 lb. *each*), peeled, if desired**
> **¼ cup olive oil or salad oil**
> **2 medium-size onions, coarsely chopped**
> **2 large green peppers, seeded and coarsely chopped**
> **3 large zucchini, cut into ½-inch-thick slices**
> **4 large tomatoes, peeled and coarsely chopped**
> **4 cloves garlic, minced or pressed**
> **1 teaspoon *each* salt, dry basil, and thyme leaves**
> **½ teaspoon oregano leaves**
> **¼ teaspoon pepper**
> **2 bay leaves**

Cut eggplants crosswise into ½-inch-thick slices, and cut each slice into quarters; set aside.

Heat oil in a 6 to 8-quart kettle over medium-high heat. Add onions and green peppers and cook, stirring, until onions are soft. Add eggplant and zucchini slices and cook, stirring often, until lightly browned.

Stir in tomatoes, garlic, salt, basil, thyme, oregano, pepper, and bay leaves. Bring to a boil. Cover, reduce heat, and cook until vegetables are almost tender when pierced (20 to 30 minutes). Uncover and boil gently, stirring occasionally, until most of the free-flowing liquid has evaporated (10 to 20 more minutes). Remove bay leaves.

Let cool; cover and refrigerate until next day or up to 4 days. Makes 6 to 8 servings.

Deviled Eggs

Plain or dressed-up, deviled eggs are basic fare that few picnickers can resist. Here we offer a standard recipe with four inviting variations to spark your own experimentation.

> **6 hard-cooked eggs, shelled and halved lengthwise**
> **3 tablespoons mayonnaise**
> **1 teaspoon Dijon mustard**
> **Salt and pepper**

Carefully remove egg yolks and place in a small bowl; set egg white halves aside. With a fork, mash yolks; stir in mayonnaise, mustard, and salt and pepper to taste. Evenly fill egg white halves with yolk mixture. Cover and refrigerate for at least 2 hours or until next day. Transport in a cooler. Makes 6 servings.

Anchovy-Celery Eggs. Prepare Deviled Eggs as directed, omitting mustard, salt, and pepper. Stir in 1 teaspoon **anchovy paste** and 6 tablespoons finely diced **celery**. Evenly fill egg white shells with yolk mixture. Slice 4 **pimento-stuffed olives** crosswise into 3 slices; lightly press an olive slice on top of each filled egg. Cover and refrigerate as directed. Transport in a cooler.

Crunchy Almond Eggs. Prepare Deviled Eggs as directed, omitting salt and pepper. Stir in 3 tablespoons chopped **salted almonds;** season to taste with **garlic salt**. Evenly fill egg white shells with yolk mixture. Lightly press a whole salted almond on top of each filled egg. Cover and refrigerate as directed. Transport in a cooler.

Oriental Deviled Eggs. Prepare Deviled Eggs as directed, omitting mustard, salt, and pepper. Stir in ½ teaspoon **soy sauce;** 2 tablespoons finely chopped **green onion**, including top; and 3 tablespoons finely chopped **water chestnuts.** Evenly fill egg white shells with yolk mixture. Lightly press a small **parsley sprig** on top of each filled egg. Cover and refrigerate as directed. Transport in a cooler.

(Continued on page 38)

Picnicking with Relish

Too often, when we hear the word "relish" we think only of a condiment for hot dogs. But relishes have many other guises and uses. They can give your picnic meal extra zest by providing piquancy and color to meat and other dishes; many relishes can also stand alone as tangy appetizers or snacks.

You can offer spiced peaches, spiced apple rings, caponata (eggplant relish), chutneys, or corn relish as toppings or trimmings for many main dishes. Marinated vegetables such as artichoke hearts, baby corn cobs, and mushrooms can be served as appetizers or side dishes. Various types of pickles, as well as pickled green tomatoes, onions, peppers, and giardiniera (pickled mixed vegetables), are popular picnic fare. And don't forget the olives—green, ripe, Greek, Sicilian, Niçoise, or any other kind that strikes your fancy.

Look for picnic relishes in delicatessens and supermarkets, or create your own fancy relishes at home—they aren't difficult to make. You can prepare the recipes below ahead of time and store them in the refrigerator until you're ready to leave; then just transport them in screw-top jars in a picnic basket. They're not spoilage-prone, and don't need to be carried in an insulated container.

English Pub-style Onions

1½ cups Madeira or port
¾ cup vinegar
½ cup firmly packed brown sugar
½ cup currants or raisins
⅛ teaspoon ground red pepper (cayenne)
3 tablespoons salad oil
2 pounds small whole white onions (¾ to 1½ inches in diameter), peeled
  Salt

In a 3 to 4-quart pan, combine Madeira, vinegar, sugar, currants, and red pepper. Bring to a boil over high heat, and continue boiling, uncovered, until reduced to 1¼ cups; set aside.

Pour oil into a large frying pan. Arrange onions in a single layer in pan, and cook over medium-high heat, shaking pan to turn onions, until lightly browned (about 7 minutes). With a slotted spoon, lift onions out and add to sauce. Brown remaining onions in the same manner and add to sauce.

Bring onion mixture to a boil over high heat. Reduce heat, cover, and simmer gently until onions are tender on outside but slightly crisp inside (10 minutes for small onions, 15 minutes for larger ones). Let cool; sprinkle with salt to taste. Cover, and refrigerate for up to 4 days. Serve onions at room temperature. Makes about 2 pints.

Bell Pepper Relish

¾ pound onions, peeled
1½ pounds (about 3 large) green or red bell peppers, seeded
1 cup white vinegar
¾ cup sugar
1½ teaspoons salt
¾ teaspoon mustard seeds

Cut onions and peppers into 1-inch chunks. Coarsely chop a portion at a time in a food processor, or put through a food chopper with a medium blade.

Place vegetables in a 2-quart pan and stir in vinegar, sugar, salt, and mustard seeds. Bring to a boil over high heat, stirring constantly. Reduce heat to medium and boil gently, uncovered, until reduced by a third; stir often. Let cool. Spoon relish into screw-top jars, cover, and refrigerate for up to 2 weeks. Makes 1½ to 2 pints.

Avocado-stuffed Eggs. Prepare Deviled Eggs as directed, omitting mayonnaise and mustard. Peel, pit, and mash 1 small **avocado** with 1 tablespoon **lemon juice.** Stir into egg yolks with 1 tablespoon finely chopped **onion** and 1½ teaspoons bottled **green taco sauce.** Evenly fill egg white shells with yolk mixture. Cover and refrigerate as directed. Transport in a cooler.

Mixed Grain Pilaf

Pilaf is a noteworthy traveler you can enjoy hot, warm, or cold. This version has a nutty flavor and a distinctive, chewy texture that can enliven almost any entrée.

⅓ cup slivered almonds
4 tablespoons butter or margarine
1 large onion, chopped
1 large carrot, shredded
1 clove garlic, minced or pressed
⅓ cup chopped parsley
⅓ cup *each* barley, brown rice, and bulgur (cracked wheat)
2½ cups regular-strength beef or chicken broth
¼ cup dry sherry or water
¾ teaspoon *each* dry basil and oregano leaves
Salt and pepper

Spread almonds in a shallow pan and toast in a 350° oven for about 8 minutes or until golden brown. Let cool completely; then place in a plastic bag to transport.

In a 3-quart pan over medium-high heat, melt butter; add onion, carrot, garlic, and parsley. Cook, stirring, until onion is soft. Add barley, rice, and bulgur; continue cooking and stirring until grains are lightly browned. Stir in broth,

sherry, basil, and oregano; bring to a boil. Cover, reduce heat, and simmer until grains are tender (45 to 55 minutes).

Remove pan from heat and let stand, covered, for 10 minutes. Season to taste with salt and pepper. To serve hot, transport as directed on page 90. To serve warm, cover and transport in a picnic basket. Or refrigerate and transport in a cooler to serve cold. Garnish with almonds. Makes 6 servings.

Simmered Black Beans

(Pictured on page 23)

Serve the beans as part of the Guatemalan appetizer party (page 5) or as a side dish with barbecued steak or hamburgers. You can purchase black beans in Mexican and Oriental markets as well as in some health food stores.

1 cup dried black beans
1 medium-size onion, finely chopped
1 small, dried whole hot red chile, crushed
½ teaspoon salt
3 cups water

Rinse beans; sort through and discard any foreign material. Drain well. Place beans in a bowl, cover with water, and let stand until next day. (Or place beans in a 2-quart pan, cover with water, and bring to a boil over high heat. Boil for 2 minutes; then remove from heat, cover, and let stand for 1 hour.)

Drain beans. In a 2-quart pan over high heat, combine beans, onion, chile, salt, and water; bring to a boil. Cover, reduce heat, and simmer until beans are very tender when pierced and most of the liquid

is absorbed (2 to 2½ hours).

If made ahead, cool, cover, and refrigerate. To reheat, place over medium heat and cook, stirring frequently, for about 15 minutes or until heated through.

Transport as directed on page 90 and serve warm. Makes 4 to 6 servings.

Quick Pinto Beans

In less than half an hour you can have this bean dish ready for the road. Wrap and carry it hot in the cooking kettle; or, if you're barbecuing, do the final heating on the grill along with steak or hamburgers.

4 strips bacon
2 large onions, coarsely chopped
1 large clove garlic, minced or pressed
½ large green pepper, seeded and chopped
1 can (10 oz.) red chili sauce
1 can (15 oz.) tomato purée
3 tablespoons firmly packed brown sugar
1 teaspoon dry mustard
3 cans (1 lb. *each*) pinto beans, drained

In a 4 or 5-quart kettle over medium heat, cook bacon until crisp. Lift out, drain, and crumble; set aside. Discard all but 2 tablespoons drippings. Add onions and garlic to pan and cook until onions are soft. Add green pepper, chili sauce, tomato purée, sugar, and mustard. Simmer, uncovered, for 15 minutes, stirring often. Stir in beans and bacon.

To transport hot, heat mixture until bubbly; remove from heat, cover, and wrap as directed on page 90. Or cover and transport; heat at picnic site just before serving. Makes 6 to 8 servings.

Indian Summer Picnic

When the air turns crisp, celebrate the changing seasons with a hearty end-of-summer picnic. Casserole Meat Loaf (page 44)—a robust mixture of beef, pork, and ham topped with crunchy pine nuts—fills the bill perfectly. Garden Vegetable Salad Bowl (page 29) is a colorful accompaniment. Finish with apples and creamy Cheesecake Cookies (page 74).

Heart of the Picnic

Distinctive main dishes to satisfy outdoor appetites

Every meal revolves around the entrée, especially at a picnic, where hearty appetites and hearty main dishes are natural partners. Because a picnic is an event rather than just a meal, your choice of entrée creates the mood and sets the pace for the entire experience. Happily, the fact that you're dining outdoors need not impose a lot of restrictions on your menu.

For the times when you don't want to bother with last-minute serving preparations, we present recipes for main dishes that are completely prepared in advance. Included is a selection of make-ahead meat dishes and savory pies, tarts, quiches, and turnovers that can be served at the picnic site with a minimum of fuss.

Other times you may want to serve main courses that require a bit of extra planning. For some, you'll need to take along sauces or relishes to be added at the last minute; others are cooked after you arrive at your destination. Even delicate or complicated main dishes can be enjoyed outdoors if you use a little planning expertise. And, after all, that's what picnicking is all about.

Bay Steak

Bay leaves not only season a tender cut of beef, but also give off a light smoke and rich aroma when they're scattered on the grill.

3 to 5 small cloves garlic
1 sirloin or porterhouse steak (about 4 lbs.), 2 inches thick
⅓ cup olive oil
8 to 10 bay leaves
Salt

Sliver 1 or 2 cloves of the garlic. Cut small gashes in steak and insert garlic slivers. Wrap steak well and refrigerate until ready to transport.

Mince or press remaining cloves garlic and combine with oil in a small screw-top jar; crumble 2 of the bay leaves and add to oil. Cover jar tightly.

Transport steak in a cooler. To cook, place steak on a grill 4 to 6 inches above a solid bed of glowing coals. Cook, turning once, for about 15 minutes on each side for rare meat or until done to your liking when slashed. Brush steak frequently with oil mixture. As meat cooks, scatter bay leaves on grill occasionally. Season steak with salt. Makes 6 to 8 servings.

Swiss Mustard Steak

A pungent mustard sauce that you prepare ahead flavors juicy slices of barbecued steak in this elegant picnic entrée. The meat is thinly sliced and swirled in the sauce before serving; remember to take along a rimmed serving platter to contain the juices.

1 clove garlic, minced or pressed
¼ cup dry vermouth or white wine
1 tablespoon Dijon mustard
¼ teaspoon Worcestershire
⅛ teaspoon *each* crushed dry rosemary, dry basil, dry tarragon, and oregano leaves
1 boneless top sirloin or top round steak, 2 to 3 inches thick
Salt and pepper

In a small bowl, stir together garlic, vermouth, mustard, and Worcestershire. Add rosemary, basil, tarragon, and oregano and stir again. Pour into a small screw-top jar and cover tightly.

Transport steak in a cooler. Cook according to directions for Bay Steak (above). When steak is almost done, pour sauce into a rimmed serving platter. Set cooked steak in sauce. Season with salt and pepper to taste.

To serve, cut meat across the grain into thin, slanting slices. Swirl each piece in sauce before transferring to individual plates. Makes 8 to 10 servings.

Steak in a Pocket

Here's a delicious main dish that's also colorful and easy to eat.

1 flank steak (1 to 1½ lbs.)
1 cup finely chopped red onion
1 cup watercress sprigs
2 tablespoons *each* chopped pimentos and chopped parsley
⅓ cup salad oil
3 tablespoons red wine vinegar
1 teaspoon dry mustard
Garlic salt and pepper
1 medium-size tomato, cut into wedges
Small romaine leaves
4 to 6 pocket breads

Broil flank steak 3 inches from heat until done to your liking (5 to 6 minutes on each side for rare). Cut steak in half lengthwise, then across grain into thin, slanting slices; let cool briefly.

In a large bowl, combine steak, onion, watercress, pimentos, and parsley. In a small bowl, stir together oil, vinegar, and mustard; stir into meat mixture. Season to taste with garlic salt and pepper. Cover and refrigerate for at least 4 hours or until next day.

Pack tomato wedges and romaine leaves in plastic bags, and transport with meat mixture in a cooler. To serve, tear or cut pocket breads in half; fill with meat mixture, tomato wedges, and romaine leaves. Makes 4 to 6 servings.

Beef Satay with Peanut Sauce

You can marinate the meat for this Indonesian-inspired dish a day ahead, but wait until you're almost ready to leave before preparing the spicy peanut sauce. At the picnic site, grill the skewered meat until done to your liking, and offer the hot sauce for dipping.

2 teaspoons curry powder
⅓ cup soy sauce
2 tablespoons *each* brown sugar, lemon juice, and salad oil
3 pounds boneless sirloin steak, cut into 1½-inch cubes
Peanut Sauce (recipe follows)

In a plastic bag, combine curry, soy, sugar, lemon juice, oil, and meat; mix well. Twist-tie bag closed and refrigerate for at least 12 hours or until next day.

(Continued on page 43)

Spectators' Special

Even confirmed landlubbers can enjoy a bright and breezy afternoon by the lake or bay, watching sailboats and picnicking on this elegant, yet portable meal. Delicately flavored Chicken Liver Pâté (page 21) spreads smoothly on crackers or chunks of French bread. Bursting under the rich golden brown crust of Vegetable Herb Pie (page 56) is a savory mélange of vegetables, rice, and cheese.

... Beef Satay (cont'd.)

Prepare Peanut Sauce and set aside. Thread meat on skewers and transport in a cooler.

To cook, place skewers on a grill about 2 inches above a solid bed of glowing coals. Cook, turning to brown all sides, for about 10 minutes for medium rare or until done to your liking when slashed.

Serve with hot sauce for dipping. Makes 6 to 8 servings.

Peanut Sauce. In a blender or food processor, combine 1 large **onion,** cut into chunks; 2 cloves **garlic;** and 1 tablespoon **water.** Whirl until smooth.

Heat 3 tablespoons **salad oil** in a small pan over low heat. Add onion mixture and cook until very soft. Stir in ¼ teaspoon **ground red pepper** (cayenne); 1 teaspoon **ground coriander;** 2 tablespoons each **brown sugar, lemon juice,** and **soy sauce;** and ¼ cup **peanut butter.** Remove from heat and gradually stir in ¾ cup **milk.** Cook over low heat, stirring constantly, until heated through. Transport in a preheated thermos (see page 90) to keep warm.

Layered Chili

(Pictured on page 50)

For a fun—and filling—main dish, choose this hearty, build-it-yourself chili. You start with a simple ground beef chili, then top it with marinated onions and other colorful relishes. The more toppings you take along, the more interesting combinations you can devise. This recipe is ideal for a tailgate party, when you have ample carrying space and want to present a really festive meal to hungry picnickers.

Pink Onions (recipe follows)
6 tablespoons salad oil
4 large onions, chopped
1 tablespoon mustard seeds
1½ pounds lean ground beef
4½ teaspoons chili powder
1 teaspoon cumin seeds
¼ teaspoon each ground cardamom and ground cinnamon
1 can (6 oz.) tomato paste
1 can (1 lb.) tomatoes
1 cup water
3 cans (about 1 lb. each) kidney beans
Relishes (suggestions follow)
3 or 4 limes, cut into wedges

Prepare Pink Onions and refrigerate.

Heat oil in an 8 to 10-quart kettle over medium-high heat; add chopped onions and cook, stirring, until soft and slightly golden. Add mustard seeds and cook, stirring, for about 1 minute. Stir in ground beef (break up with a spoon) and cook, stirring occasionally, until meat is lightly browned.

Add chili powder, cumin seeds, cardamom, cinnamon, tomato paste, and tomatoes (break up with a spoon) and their liquid. Pour in water and beans. Simmer rapidly, uncovered, until most of the liquid has evaporated and chili is thickened (about 40 minutes); stir frequently to prevent scorching. If made ahead, cool slightly, cover loosely, and refrigerate; reheat, adding water to prevent sticking, if necessary.

Wrap and transport chili as directed on page 90. Transport Pink Onions and relishes in a cooler. To serve, ladle hot chili into bowls, and top with Pink Onions and relishes as desired. Squeeze on lime juice to taste. Makes 6 servings.

Pink Onions. In a 2 to 3-quart pan over high heat, bring 4 cups **water** and 3 tablespoons **vinegar** to a boil. Add

2 large **red onions,** thinly sliced, and push down into liquid. Return to a boil and cook, uncovered, for 2 to 3 minutes. Drain well and let cool.

In a large bowl, combine onions with 1 tablespoon **vinegar,** 2 tablespoons **salad oil,** 1 teaspoon **mustard seeds,** ½ teaspoon **cumin seeds,** and **salt** to taste. Cover loosely with foil and refrigerate until well chilled. Transport in a cooler. Makes about 2 cups.

Relishes. Choose at least 5 from this list: 3 medium-size **tomatoes,** chopped; 1 can (7 oz.) chopped **green chiles;** 1 medium-size **cucumber,** chopped; 1 cup sliced **green onions** (including tops) or diced onions; 1 pint (2 cups) **sour cream;** 2 cups (8 oz.) shredded **jack** or Cheddar **cheese;** 2 **green peppers,** diced; 2 to 3 cups shredded **iceberg lettuce;** 2 **avocados,** peeled, pitted, diced, and mixed with 3 tablespoons **lemon juice;** and bottled Mexican-style **hot sauce** (red or green). Pack in individual containers and transport in a cooler.

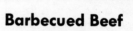

Barbecued Beef Sandwiches

(Pictured on page 58)

A Dutch oven is not only a reliable cooking utensil, but also an ideal container for carrying a hot entrée—such as this zesty meat sandwich filling—to a cool-weather picnic.

Once you arrive at the picnic site, take the Dutch oven out of its foil and newspaper wrapping and let guests spoon the hot beef and sauce into soft rolls. If you prefer, substitute seeded buns for the onion rolls.

(Continued on next page)

. . .Beef Sandwiches (cont'd.)

    2 tablespoons salad oil

    4 to 5-pound cross-rib or sirloin
      tip roast or lean, boneless,
      rolled and tied leg or loin pork
      roast

    2 large onions, chopped

    1 large green pepper, seeded
      and chopped

    2 stalks celery, chopped

    2 large cloves garlic, minced or
      pressed

    1 cup catsup

    1 can (1 lb.) stewed tomatoes

    ¼ cup cider vinegar

    ⅓ cup firmly packed brown
      sugar

    1 teaspoon chili powder

    ½ teaspoon *each* dry basil,
      oregano leaves, ground
      cinnamon, salt, and liquid
      smoke

    8 to 10 onion rolls, halved

Heat oil in a 6 to 8-quart Dutch oven over medium-high heat. Add meat and cook until browned on all sides; remove from pan and set aside.

Reduce heat to medium and add onions, green pepper, celery, and garlic. Cook until onions are limp. Add catsup, tomatoes, vinegar, brown sugar, and chili powder. Then stir in basil, oregano, cinnamon, salt, and liquid smoke. Simmer, uncovered, for about 10 minutes.

Return meat to pan and spoon sauce over it. Cover and bake in a 325° oven for about 3 hours or until meat is tender when pierced. Let cool slightly, cover loosely, and refrigerate until next day. (Do not refrigerate in a cast-iron pot.)

About 2 hours before departure, spoon off and discard congealed fat, lift out meat, and thinly slice. Return sliced meat to pan, layering it with sauce. Cover and heat in a 350° oven for about 55 minutes or until hot and bubbly. Transport as directed on page 90.

Serve within 4 hours, spooning meat and sauce into onion rolls. Makes 8 to 10 servings.

Casserole Meat Loaf

(Pictured on page 39)

Pine nuts and chunks of diced ham accent this decorative, French-style meat loaf. You can carry it to the picnic in its baking dish; when you're ready to eat, just slice and serve with crusty bread.

    3 tablespoons butter or
      margarine

    1 medium-size onion, finely
      chopped

    ¼ pound mushrooms, finely
      chopped

    ¼ cup brandy or sherry

    3 eggs

    ½ cup condensed consommé

    4 slices fresh white bread, torn
      into pieces

    2 cloves garlic

    ½ teaspoon *each* thyme leaves
      and ground allspice

    ½ teaspoon salt

    1½ pounds lean ground beef

    1 pound ground pork

    ½ pound cooked ham, sliced ½
      inch thick

    ⅔ cup pine nuts

In a large frying pan over medium heat, melt 2 tablespoons of the butter. Add onion and cook until glazed; add mushrooms and remaining 1 tablespoon butter and cook, stirring, for about 1 minute. Add brandy, reduce heat, and simmer for 1 minute. Let cool.

In a blender or food processor, place eggs, consommé, bread, garlic, thyme, allspice, and salt; whirl until smooth.

Place ground meats in a large bowl; stir in onion and egg mixtures. Cut ham into ½-inch cubes and stir into meat mixture along with ⅓ cup of the pine nuts. Turn into a greased 1½ or 2-quart casserole, and sprinkle remaining nuts on top.

Bake, uncovered, in a 325° oven for 1½ hours or until well

browned. Let cool slightly, cover loosely with foil, and refrigerate until next day. Remove any congealed fat from sides. Transport in a cooler. To serve, remove from casserole and cut into ½-inch-thick slices. Makes 10 to 12 servings.

Empanadas

(Pictured on page 26)

In Latin American countries, the savory turnovers called *empanadas* come in all shapes, sizes, and flavors. Here's a hearty, main-dish version with a spicy meat filling that can be made with lamb, beef, or pork. Wrapped well, the empanadas stay warm for up to 3 hours.

    About 2 pounds bone-in lamb
      shoulder, beef chuck, or pork
      shoulder steaks, about ¾ inch
      thick

    2 tablespoons all-purpose flour

    2 tablespoons salad oil

    1 large onion, finely chopped

    2 cloves garlic, minced or
      pressed

    2 teaspoons ground coriander

    1½ teaspoons *each* chili powder
      and salt

    ¼ to ½ teaspoon ground red
      pepper (cayenne)

    2¼ cups water

    1 small russet potato

    1 small can (2¼ oz.) sliced ripe
      olives, drained

    ½ cup *each* raisins, chopped
      parsley, and frozen peas

    4½ cups baking mix (biscuit mix)

    1 cup water

    1 egg

    1 tablespoon water

Cut meat from bone; trim off excess fat. Cut meat into ¾-inch cubes (you should have about 4 cups). In a bag, combine meat and flour; shake until coated.

Heat oil in a wide frying pan over medium heat. Add meat about a third at a time, and cook, stirring, until lightly browned. Push meat to one side and add onion, garlic, coriander, chili powder, salt, and red pepper. Cook, stirring, until onion is soft. Add the 2¼ cups water, scraping up browned bits from pan bottom. Bring to a boil; cover, reduce heat, and simmer until meat is almost tender (30 to 40 minutes).

Peel potato and cut into ¾-inch cubes. Add to meat mixture; cover and simmer until potato is almost tender (15 to 20 minutes). Add olives, raisins, parsley, and peas. Cover and simmer until peas are tender (about 10 minutes); let cool. (At this point, you may cover and refrigerate until next day.)

In a bowl, stir together baking mix and the 1 cup water to form a soft dough. Divide dough into 8 equal pieces; knead each piece into a ball. On a lightly floured board, roll each portion into an 8-inch circle. Place about ⅛ of the meat filling in center of each circle. Bring edges together on top of filling, lightly moisten with water, and pinch to seal. Flute decoratively.

With a spatula, place pies an inch apart on ungreased baking sheets. With a fork, prick top of each pie. In a small bowl, beat egg with the 1 tablespoon water, and brush egg mixture over pies.

Bake in a 400° oven for 25 to 30 minutes or until firm and golden brown. Transfer to racks and let cool slightly. To carry, wrap and transport as directed on page 90.

If made ahead, let cool completely; then wrap each pie in foil and refrigerate for up to 2 days. To reheat, bake, uncovered, in a 350° oven for 15 minutes or until heated through. Makes 8 servings.

Veal with Tuna Sauce

Known in Italy as *vitello tonnato*, this classic Italian dish makes elegant summer picnic fare. Simmered veal is thinly sliced, then marinated in tuna sauce and served cold. For a more economical version, substitute turkey for the veal.

Tuna Sauce (recipe follows)
4 to 5 pounds veal leg or shoulder, or turkey breast, boned, rolled, and tied
1½ cups dry white wine
1 large carrot, sliced
1 stalk celery, sliced
1 small onion, chopped
1 bay leaf
6 parsley sprigs
1 clove garlic, minced or pressed
Lemon slices, anchovy fillets, ripe olives, capers, and parsley sprigs

Prepare Tuna Sauce and refrigerate.

In a 5 to 6-quart kettle or Dutch oven, place veal, wine, carrot, celery, onion, bay leaf, the 6 parsley sprigs, and garlic. Pour in enough water just to cover meat. Bring to a boil over high heat; cover, reduce heat, and simmer until meat is tender when pierced or a meat thermometer inserted in thickest part registers 170° (1½ to 2 hours). Let meat cool in cooking liquid; then cover and refrigerate until well chilled.

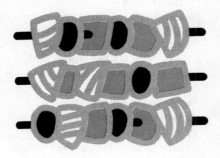

Remove meat from liquid (strain liquid and reserve for other uses); slice meat thinly. Pour a third of the Tuna Sauce into a large, shallow serving dish. Arrange meat slices in dish and cover with remaining sauce. Cover and refrigerate for at least 2 hours or until next day. Transport in a cooler. Pack lemon slices, anchovies, olives, capers, and parsley separately; use to garnish meat before serving. Makes about 12 servings.

Tuna Sauce. Drain oil from 1 small can (about 3 oz.) **tuna** into a measuring cup. Add enough **olive oil** or salad oil to make 1 cup.

In a blender or food processor, combine tuna, 5 **anchovy fillets,** 3 tablespoons **lemon juice,** 2 **eggs,** and 1½ tablespoons **capers;** whirl until smooth. With motor on high, gradually add oil in a thin, steady stream until sauce is thickened and well blended. Cover and refrigerate for up to a week. Makes about 1½ cups.

Plum-flavored Ribs

Marinate slabs of pork spareribs in a sweet sauce; then grill them slowly until they're plump and juicy. The plum marinade is equally good with beef ribs or lamb riblets.

3 tablespoons soy sauce
1 cup dry red wine
¼ cup *each* red wine vinegar and salad oil
⅓ cup plum jam
2 cloves garlic, minced or pressed
1 medium-size onion, finely chopped
½ teaspoon thyme leaves
8 pounds lean pork spareribs, left uncut in whole slabs

(Continued on next page)

In a small pan over medium heat, combine soy, wine, vinegar, oil, jam, garlic, onion, and thyme. Stir until bubbling; let cool.

Put a large plastic bag in a rimmed baking pan. Place rib slabs in bag, pour in marinade, and twist-tie bag closed. Refrigerate for at least 4 hours or until next day, turning bag over occasionally. Transport in a cooler.

To cook, remove ribs from bag, reserving marinade. Place meat on a grill 4 to 6 inches above a solid bed of low-glowing coals. Cook, turning and basting frequently with remaining marinade, for about 1 hour or until meat near bone is no longer pink when slashed. To serve, cut into individual ribs. Makes about 8 servings.

Mustardy Sausage Sandwiches

Even several hours after you leave home, you can enjoy hot and hearty sausage sandwiches. You'll need a Dutch oven with a tight-fitting lid; well wrapped, the pan keeps the filling warm for up to 4 hours.

4 tablespoons butter or margarine

5 large onions (about 2½ lbs. *total*), sliced

2 cloves garlic, minced or pressed

3 tablespoons flour

1½ cups regular-strength chicken broth

¼ cup *each* catsup and Dijon mustard

2 tablespoons prepared horseradish

10 to 12 (about 3 lbs. *total*) kielbasa (Polish sausage)

10 to 12 French rolls

In a 5 or 6-quart Dutch oven with a tight-fitting lid, melt 3

tablespoons of the butter over medium heat. Add onions and garlic; cover and cook, stirring often, until onions are very soft (about 10 minutes). Uncover and cook, stirring, until mixture is bubbly.
and cook, stirring often, until onions are golden (about 20 more minutes). Sprinkle in flour and cook, stirring, until bubbly.

Gradually add chicken broth; cook, stirring, until sauce boils and thickens. Stir in catsup, mustard, and horseradish. Remove from heat.

Meanwhile, in a wide frying pan over medium heat, melt remaining 1 tablespoon butter. Add kielbasa and cook until browned; drain. Add sausages to sauce. If made ahead, cool slightly, cover loosely, and refrigerate for up to 2 days; reheat, covered, in a 350° oven for about 55 minutes or until bubbly and heated through.

Wrap and transport as directed on page 90. Serve within 4 hours, spooning sausage filling into French rolls. Makes 10 to 12 servings.

Baked Beans Olé

Bake hearty pork and beans with sliced sausage and green chiles, and top with French-fried onions. Then, at the picnic site, spoon the hot bean mixture into warm, soft tortillas to eat out of hand.

1 large can (3 lbs. 5 oz.) pork and beans

¼ cup firmly packed brown sugar

¼ cup chopped parsley

1 can (4 oz.) diced green chiles

3 or 4 (about 1 lb. *total*) kielbasa (Polish sausage), sliced

½ teaspoon chili powder

¼ teaspoon ground cumin

12 to 16 corn or flour tortillas

1 can (3 oz.) French-fried onions

In a 2-quart casserole, stir together pork and beans, sugar, parsley, diced chiles, sausage slices, chili powder, and cumin. Bake, uncovered, in a 350° oven for 35 minutes or until heated through; stir several times.

Meanwhile, dampen your hands with water, pat each tortilla, and then pile in 2 equal stacks. Wrap each stack in foil and warm in oven during last 15 minutes bean mixture is baking.

When bean mixture is hot, sprinkle onions evenly over top and bake for 3 to 5 more minutes or until onions are lightly browned. Cover. Wrap casserole and foil-covered tortillas and transport as directed on page 90.

To serve, spoon some of the bean mixture into each tortilla. Makes 6 to 8 servings.

Spiced Pork Roll

Accompany this cold pork roll with a flavorful herb mayonnaise; another time, spread the mayonnaise on bread for sandwiches. You can prepare the meat up to a week in advance; slice it thinly to serve.

1 pork loin roast (about 5 lbs.), boned

½ teaspoon *each* ground allspice, pepper, and sugar

1 teaspoon salt

6 to 8 whole cloves

4 cups water

2 carrots, sliced

1 medium-size onion, sliced

8 to 10 *each* black peppercorns and whole allspice

Herb Mayonnaise (recipe follows)

Trim off and discard fat from meat. In a small bowl, stir together ground allspice, pepper,

Nomads' Feast

If any people are experts in picnicking, it must be the nomadic Bedouins of the Middle East. And their festival lamb dish, Mansef (page 48), is a natural picnic centerpiece. Flavored with cinnamon, cloves, and pine nuts, the lamb and rice stew is spooned into warm tortillas in our version. For dessert, lemon-scented Almond Cake (page 77) lends piquancy, along with fresh fruits and pistachios.

... Spiced Pork Roll (cont'd.)

sugar, and salt; rub into all sides of meat.

Form meat into a compact loaf; using string, tie crosswise and lengthwise at 1-inch intervals. Stud meat with cloves. Place roll in a 4 to 5-quart pan; add water, carrots, onion, peppercorns, and whole allspice. Bring to a boil over high heat. Cover, reduce heat, and simmer for 1½ hours, turning meat over once or twice.

Remove pan from heat and place a flat plate or pie pan slightly smaller than cooking pan directly on meat. Place a weight (such as a heavy can) on plate to press down surface. Refrigerate until next day.

Prepare Herb Mayonnaise and refrigerate.

Remove meat from broth (reserve broth for other uses) and cut away string. Wrap in plastic wrap. If made ahead, refrigerate meat for up to a week. Transport meat in a cooler. To serve, slice meat thinly and pass Herb Mayonnaise to spoon over individual servings. Makes 10 to 12 servings.

Herb Mayonnaise. In a blender or food processor, combine ¼ cup lightly packed chopped **parsley,** ¼ cup chopped **chives,** ¼ teaspoon **dill weed,** 4 teaspoons **lemon juice,** and ½ cup **mayonnaise.** Whirl until smoothly blended. Pour into a container, cover, and refrigerate for at least 3 hours. Transport in a cooler. Makes about ½ cup.

Glazed Ham Loaf

Slices of baked ham loaf get an extra flavor boost when accompanied by a creamy, piquant horseradish sauce. Offer the ham warm or cold.

Horseradish Sauce (recipe follows)
2 pounds uncooked smoked ham, ground
1½ pounds ground pork
1 cup cracker crumbs
2 eggs
1 cup hot milk
1 cup spiced peach syrup

Prepare Horseradish Sauce several hours ahead of time, and refrigerate.

In a large bowl, combine ham, pork, cracker crumbs, and eggs; mix well. Stir in milk. Shape into a loaf and place in center of a 9-inch square pan. Pour over as much peach syrup as will soak into loaf.

Bake in a 350° oven for 45 minutes, basting several times with remaining syrup. To serve warm, wrap in foil and transport as directed on page 90. To serve cold, let cool slightly, cover loosely with foil, and refrigerate until well chilled; transport in a cooler.

Serve with Horseradish Sauce. Makes 8 servings.

Horseradish Sauce. In a large bowl, beat ½ cup **whipping cream** until stiff; fold in 1 tablespoon **prepared horseradish,** 1 teaspoon **sugar,** and ½ teaspoon **lemon juice.** Spoon into a container, cover, and refrigerate for at least 3 hours or until next day. Transport in a cooler. Makes about 1 cup.

Mansef

(Pictured on page 47)

The nomadic Bedouins of northern Africa and southwestern Asia enjoy a one-dish meal of lamb, rice, and pine nuts called *mansef*. Here, it has been adapted for picnic use during your own nomadic wanderings.

4 pounds boneless lamb (shoulder roast or leg)
6 cups water
2 teaspoons salt
2 whole cinnamon sticks
10 whole cloves
2 large packages (8 oz. *each*) cream cheese
5 tablespoons lemon juice
About 4 tablespoons butter or margarine
1 cup pine nuts
16 flour tortillas
Hot Cooked Rice (recipe follows)
Mint sprigs and lemon wedges

Trim off and discard fat from lamb; cut meat into 1 to 1½-inch cubes. Place in a 5-quart Dutch oven with water, salt, cinnamon, and cloves. Bring to a boil over high heat; cover, reduce heat, and simmer for 1 hour.

Skim off and discard as much fat as possible. Ladle out 3 cups of the meat juices and pour into the large bowl of an electric mixer or into a blender container.

Blend the 3 cups juices with cream cheese until smooth; return cheese mixture to pan. Add lemon juice and continue to simmer, covered, until meat is very tender when pierced. (At this point, you may cool, cover, and refrigerate until next day. Reheat to continue.)

In a wide frying pan over medium heat, melt about 2 tablespoons of the butter. Add nuts and cook, stirring constantly, until lightly browned (*do not scorch*). Let cool; transport in a plastic bag.

Lightly dot tortillas with remaining butter and pile in 2 equal stacks. Wrap each stack in foil and warm in center of a 350° oven for 10 to 15 minutes.

Prepare Hot Cooked Rice. Lay heated tortillas, well wrapped in foil, on top of rice to keep them warm; then replace lid. Transport as directed on page 90.

Pour hot juices from meat into a preheated thermos (see page 90). Transport Dutch oven as directed on page 90. Take a serving platter along, too.

To serve, spoon hot rice onto platter. Spoon meat over rice and pour some of the hot juices over all. Sprinkle with pine nuts. Keep mansef hot by pouring on steaming juices as needed. Cut tortillas in half, fold, and arrange around rim of platter. Garnish with mint and lemon wedges.

To eat, spoon a little mansef onto half a tortilla, fold, and eat out of hand; or offer forks and plates. Makes 8 servings.

Hot Cooked Rice. In a large pan over high heat, bring about 3 quarts **water** to a boil. Add 2 cups **rice** and 2 teaspoons **salt.** Cover, reduce heat, and simmer until rice is tender (about 15 minutes).

Roast Chicken with Herbs

(Pictured on page 78)

Buttery, garlic-scented roast chicken with herbs is a classic French specialty that can be made a day ahead and served cold.

    2 broiler-fryer chickens (about 3 lbs. *each*)
    2 cloves garlic, cut in half
    4 bay leaves
    4 whole cloves garlic, peeled
    6 tablespoons butter or margarine, melted
    1 teaspoon *each* salt and pepper
    ½ teaspoon *each* thyme, oregano, and marjoram leaves; ground sage; and dry basil
    Watercress sprigs (optional)

Remove giblets from chickens and reserve for other uses.

Rub skin of each chicken with 1 clove of cut garlic. Then stuff each body cavity with 2 of the bay leaves and 3 cloves of the garlic (including cut ones).

In a small bowl, stir together butter, salt, pepper, thyme, oregano, marjoram, sage, and basil. Spoon 1 tablespoon of the butter mixture into body cavity of each chicken. Tie legs of each chicken together. Brush chickens generously with butter mixture.

Place chickens, breast side down, on a rack in a shallow roasting pan. Place in a cold oven; then turn oven to 425°. Bake for 45 minutes. Turn chickens breast side up and continue baking, basting occasionally with any remaining butter mixture or pan drippings, for 40 to 45 more minutes or until juices run clear and meat near thigh bone is no longer pink when slashed.

Let cool slightly, cover loosely with foil, and refrigerate until well chilled or until next day. Transport in a cooler. To serve, cut into pieces with poultry shears. Garnish with watercress, if desired. Makes 6 to 8 servings.

Breadbasket Chicken

For a portable meal that's ready to travel in less than an hour, tuck a spit-roasted chicken inside a loaf of brown-and-serve bread; the chicken heats as the bread bakes. Then just wrap the whole loaf in foil and newspaper for a warm—and hearty—picnic entrée.

    1 round loaf brown-and-serve French bread (1½ lbs.)
    ½ cup (¼ lb.) butter or margarine, melted
    ½ teaspoon oregano leaves
    2 green onions (including tops), thinly sliced
    1 or 2 spit or oven-roasted chickens (about 2 lbs. *each*)

Cut loaf of bread in half horizontally. Scoop out soft bread from top and bottom halves, leaving a shell ½ to ¾ inch thick. (Reserve soft bread for other uses, if desired.)

In a small bowl, combine butter, oregano, and onions. Evenly brush butter mixture over inside of bread shells.

Quarter chicken and arrange in bottom bread shell. Cover with top shell and place loaf on a large piece of heavy-duty foil.

Bake, uncovered, in a 400° oven for 25 minutes or until bread is richly browned and crisp. Remove from oven and wrap foil around loaf to enclose completely. Transport as directed on page 90. To serve, remove top of bread, lift out chicken pieces, and cut bread into slices or wedges. Makes 4 to 8 servings.

Spinach-stuffed Chicken Breasts

Stuff boned chicken breasts with a savory spinach filling to create a fancy picnic entrée. You can serve the breasts whole, or cut them crosswise into inch-thick slices to display the vivid green filling.

(Continued on page 51)

Tailgate Chili Party

On a nippy football day—or any other time a tailgate picnic is called for—serve Layered Chili (page 43). Bowls of this thick beef and tomato-based chili invite topping with cool sour cream, avocado chunks, marinated red onions, and other condiments. Add to the pregame festivities with pitchers of beer from a small keg, and a big basket of autumn fruits and nuts.

50

... Chicken Breasts (cont'd.)

- **8 strips bacon**
- **1 large onion, finely chopped**
- **1 package (10 oz.) frozen chopped spinach, thawed, with liquid squeezed out**
- **1 egg, lightly beaten**
- **½ cup seasoned croutons, lightly crushed**
- **½ teaspoon garlic salt**
- **4 whole chicken breasts (about 1 lb. *each*), split, skinned, and boned**
- **Salt and pepper**
- **3 tablespoons salad oil**

In a wide frying pan over medium heat, cook bacon until crisp. Remove bacon from pan, drain, and crumble; set aside. Discard all but 2 tablespoons drippings.

Add onion to pan and cook until soft (about 10 minutes). Remove pan from heat and stir in spinach, egg, croutons, garlic salt, and bacon.

With a sharp knife, cut a pocket in thick side of each chicken breast half. Stuff with spinach mixture and close with a wooden pick. Sprinkle chicken lightly with salt and pepper.

Heat oil in a wide frying pan over medium heat. Add chicken breasts and cook, turning to brown all sides, until meat in thickest portion is no longer pink when slashed (12 to 15 minutes).

Remove chicken and drain on paper towels. Let cool slightly, cover loosely with foil, and refrigerate until well chilled. Transport in a cooler. Makes 8 servings.

Crusty Parmesan Chicken

(Pictured on page 91)

For chicken that's crunchy and delicious hot or cold, try this quick and easy oven-fried version. The recipe multiplies easily to feed a crowd.

- **1 cup dry bread crumbs**
- **½ cup grated Parmesan cheese**
- **½ teaspoon *each* paprika and garlic salt**
- **¼ teaspoon pepper**
- **2 tablespoons chopped parsley**
- **4 tablespoons butter or margarine**
- **1 broiler-fryer chicken (about 3 lbs.), cut into pieces**

In a medium-size bowl, stir together bread crumbs, Parmesan cheese, paprika, garlic salt, pepper, and parsley.

In a pan over medium heat, melt butter. Dip chicken in butter, then roll in crumb mixture. Place chicken, skin side up, in a lightly greased baking pan, arranging pieces so they do not touch.

Bake in a 350° oven for 1 hour or until meat near thigh bone is no longer pink when slashed. To serve warm, wrap in foil and transport as directed on page 90. To serve cold, let cool slightly, cover loosely with foil, and refrigerate until well chilled. Transport in a cooler. Makes 4 or 5 servings.

Papaya Turkey Salad

(Pictured on page 15)

Enjoying a creative picnic when carrying space is limited, as on a bicycling trip, presents a real challenge. Here's one solution: buy the ingredients at the supermarket just before mealtime.

- **1 large papaya or cantaloupe**
- **1 can (5 oz.) boned turkey or chicken**
- **1 lime**
- **½ pint (1 cup) peach or apricot-flavored yogurt**

Just before eating, cut papaya in half and scoop out seeds. Fill center of each half with turkey. As you eat, squeeze lime and spoon yogurt over top. Makes 2 servings.

Overnight Layered Chicken Salad

Spread a curry-flavored dressing over layers of crisp vegetables and chicken for this make-ahead salad. When you serve it, scoop down to the bottom of the dish so everyone gets a portion of each layer.

- **6 cups shredded iceberg lettuce**
- **¼ pound bean sprouts**
- **1 can (8 oz.) water chestnuts, drained and sliced**
- **½ cup thinly sliced green onions (including tops)**
- **1 medium-size cucumber, thinly sliced**
- **About 4 cups cooked chicken, cut into 2 to 3-inch strips**
- **2 packages (6 oz. *each*) frozen Chinese pea pods, thawed**
- **2 cups mayonnaise**
- **2 teaspoons curry powder**
- **1 tablespoon sugar**
- **½ teaspoon ground ginger**
- **½ cup Spanish peanuts**
- **12 to 18 cherry tomatoes, halved**

Spread lettuce evenly in a shallow 4-quart serving dish. Top with bean sprouts, water chestnuts, onions, cucumber, and chicken. Pat pea pods dry and arrange on top.

In a small bowl, stir together mayonnaise, curry, sugar, and ginger. Spread mayonnaise mixture evenly over pea pods. Cover and refrigerate until well chilled or until next day.

Transport in a cooler. Just before serving, garnish with peanuts and tomato halves. Makes 10 to 12 servings.

The Picnicker's Guide to American Wines

Perhaps Omar Khayyám said it best: "A book of verses underneath the bough, a jug of wine, a loaf of bread—and thou. . . ." There's no denying the pleasure of enjoying wine in an outdoor setting, especially when the wine is carefully chosen to enhance the food being served.

To help you select the right wine for your picnic menu, here's a quick guide to some commonly available American wines. It's intended primarily as a source of inspiration. Experiment to find the wines you prefer; then try combining them with different foods.

A tip for keeping wine cold on a picnic: put the bottle in a container of ice water, rather than in ice alone. This keeps the wine colder and makes it easier to replace the bottle after filling your glass.

White wines

For a light and fruity wine, often with a hint of sweetness, try White Riesling (Johannisberg Riesling), Chenin Blanc, Gewürtztraminer, French Colombard, Grey Riesling, or Chablis. Keep these wines iced and serve them with lightly seasoned fish, shellfish, and poultry dishes; ham; and cold salads.

The more full-bodied, flavorful white wines, usually dry, include Chardonnay (Pinot Chardonnay), Pinot Blanc, Sauvignon Blanc (Fumé Blanc), dry Chenin Blanc, and generic white table wines. In general, these go well with more heavily seasoned fish, shellfish, and poultry dishes; deli meats; and cheeses. Serve them cold or at room temperature.

Blanc de Noir wines

These white wines, made from black grapes, include Petite Sirah Blanc, Zinfandel Blanc, Cabernet Sauvignon Blanc, and Pinot Noir Blanc. Sometimes dry but usually slightly sweet, they range in color from pale salmon to light copper. Serve them iced with chicken, game, ham, veal, or quiche.

Rosé wines

Rosé wines, served cold, may be offered as apéritifs, and they go well with such foods as ham, quiche, cold cuts, and hot dogs. These light red wines are generic blends—that is, they are made from an assortment of grapes. Rosé wines have a fruity flavor ranging from slightly sweet to sweet.

Red wines

Fresh and fruity light-bodied red wines, dry or just off-dry, can be served at room temperature or lightly chilled. These wines—Gamay, Gamay Beaujolais, Zinfandel, and Burgundy— are excellent accompaniments to chicken, cold meats, stews, charcoal-grilled meats, quiche, and pasta salads.

For a more full-bodied red wine with distinctive flavor, choose Barbera, Petite Sirah, Merlot, Zinfandel, Cabernet Sauvignon, or Pinot Noir. These wines are served at room temperature with full-flavored foods such as beef, lamb, and game.

Sparkling wines

Ranging from ultradry to very sweet, sparkling wines are served chilled as apéritifs, with brunch, with light entrées such as chicken and veal, or with dessert. They may be labeled Natural (very dry), Brut (dry), Extra Dry (hint of sweetness), Dry (medium sweet), Sec (noticeably sweet), or Demi-Sec (very sweet). These wines include Blanc de Blanc (white champagne made from white grapes), Blanc de Noir (white champagne made from black grapes), Pink Champagne (usually sweet), Sparkling Burgundy and Champagne Rouge (red, usually off-dry).

Cheesy Chicken & Ham Bundles

Serve these pastry-wrapped bundles of chicken, ham, and cheese warm or cold for easy eating out of hand. You can poach the chicken a day ahead and refrigerate the boned breasts until ready to use.

- 3 **whole chicken breasts (about 1 lb. *each*), split**
- ¼ **cup dry sherry**
- 1 **chicken bouillon cube dissolved in 1 cup hot water**
- ⅓ **cup prepared mustard**
- ¾ **teaspoon garlic salt**
- ¾ **teaspoon fines herbes or ¼ teaspoon *each* sage leaves, dry basil, and thyme leaves**
- 6 **slices (about 4 by 6 inches) jack cheese**
- 6 **thin slices (about 4 by 6 inches) cooked ham**
- 1 **package (10 oz.) frozen patty shells**
- 1 **egg white**
  Poppy or sesame seeds (optional)

Place chicken breasts in a 3-quart pan; pour sherry and bouillon mixture over chicken. Bring to a boil over high heat; cover, reduce heat, and simmer until chicken is tender when pierced (about 20 minutes). Let cool in broth for 30 minutes; then lift out chicken (reserve broth for other uses), and remove and discard skin and bones. Refrigerate chicken for several hours or until next day.

In a small bowl, stir together mustard, garlic salt, and fines herbes until blended. Spread 1 tablespoon of the mustard mixture over each piece of chicken, coating thoroughly. Wrap a slice of cheese and then a slice of ham around each piece.

Let patty shells stand at room temperature for 30 min-
utes. On a lightly floured board, roll each shell into an 8-inch circle. Place a piece of the wrapped chicken, seam side down, in center of each pastry circle. Bring up sides of pastry and overlap in center; moisten and pinch to seal. Fold up ends of pastry; moisten and pinch to seal.

Place bundles, seam side down, at least 2 inches apart on an ungreased baking sheet. In a small bowl, beat egg white and brush over pastry; sprinkle with poppy seeds, if desired. Refrigerate for 30 minutes.

Bake in a 425° oven for 30 minutes or until richly browned and crisp. Transfer bundles to a rack and let cool for 20 minutes. To serve warm, wrap and transport as directed on page 90. To serve cold, cover loosely with foil and refrigerate until well chilled. Transport in a cooler. Makes 6 servings.

Picnic Meat Pies

Chile and cheese-flavored meat pies are easy to serve and eat almost anywhere. If you prefer a milder-tasting version, you can reduce the number of chiles or omit them altogether.

- 1 **chicken breast (about ¾ lb.)**
- ½ **pound bulk pork sausage**
- 1 **medium-size onion, chopped**
- 1 **large clove garlic, minced or pressed**
- ⅓ **cup sour cream mixed with 1 teaspoon all-purpose flour**
- 1 **large can (7 oz.) diced green chiles, drained**
- 1 **cup (4 oz.) shredded sharp Cheddar cheese**
- 3 **cups baking mix (biscuit mix)**
- ⅔ **cup water**
- 1 **egg yolk**
- 1 **tablespoon water**

Place chicken breast in a small pan and pour in enough water to cover. Bring to a boil over high heat; cover, reduce heat, and simmer until chicken is tender when pierced (about 15 minutes). Let cool in broth; then lift out chicken (reserve broth for other uses), and remove and discard skin and bones. Shred meat and set aside.

In a wide frying pan over medium heat, brown sausage. Add onion and garlic, and cook, stirring, until onion is limp. Remove from heat; stir in chicken, sour cream mixture, chiles, and cheese until blended. (At this point, you may cover and refrigerate until next day.)

In a bowl, stir together baking mix and the ⅔ cup water to form a soft dough. Divide dough into thirds. On a lightly floured board, roll each portion into a 10-inch square; cut each into 4 equal 5-inch squares. Place ¼ cup of the meat filling in each square; fold corner to corner over filling to form a triangle. Pinch edges to seal.

Place meat pies an inch apart on lightly greased baking sheets; with a knife, cut several slashes in top of each pie. In a small bowl, beat egg yolk with the 1 tablespoon water, and brush egg mixture over crusts.

Bake in a 350° oven for 20 minutes or until golden brown. Transfer pies to racks and let cool slightly. Wrap and transport as directed on page 90. Makes 12 pies.

Poached Salmon Steaks with Asparagus

(Pictured on page 55)

Delicate shades of pink and green lend understated

elegance to this light—and splendid—summer picnic entrée for two. A green mayonnaise complements both the salmon and the asparagus.

- 1 quart water
- 1 medium-size onion, sliced
- 6 black peppercorns
- 1 bay leaf
- 1 teaspoon salt
- ¾ to 1 pound asparagus
- 2 salmon steaks, *each* about 1 inch thick
  Lemon slices, capers, parsley sprigs, and tomato wedges for garnishes
  Green Butter Mayonnaise (recipe follows)

In a frying pan over high heat, combine water, onion, peppercorns, bay leaf, and salt. Bring to a boil; cover, reduce heat, and simmer for 15 minutes.

Meanwhile, snap off and discard tough ends of asparagus. Add asparagus to frying pan and simmer, uncovered, just until tender when pierced (6 to 8 minutes). With tongs, remove asparagus, rinse under cold water, drain well, and set aside. If made ahead, let cool; then cover and refrigerate.

Add salmon steaks to pan; cover and simmer in stock until just pink throughout (8 to 10 minutes). With a slotted spatula, remove steaks and drain briefly. Let cool slightly, cover loosely with foil, and refrigerate until well chilled. Pack lemon slices, capers, parsley, and tomatoes in plastic bags.

Prepare Green Butter Mayonnaise and transport with salmon and garnishes in a cooler. To serve, top each salmon steak with a lemon slice, capers, and parsley; serve with asparagus. Garnish each plate with tomato; pass Green Butter Mayonnaise. Makes 2 servings.

Green Butter Mayonnaise. Assemble ⅔ cup firmly packed chopped fresh **spinach** and 2 tablespoons chopped **parsley.**

In a small pan over low heat, melt ⅓ cup **butter** or margarine. Meanwhile, in a blender or food processor, combine 2 **egg yolks,** ¼ teaspoon **salt,** 1 tablespoon **lemon juice,** and ½ teaspoon **dry tarragon;** whirl briefly.

When butter is melted and bubbling, turn blender on high and add butter in a slow, steady stream. Then add ¼ cup **salad oil** in a slow, steady stream. (If sauce becomes too thick before all the oil has been added, blend in some of the spinach and then add remaining oil.)

Add parsley and remaining spinach; whirl until greens are finely chopped and well combined. Pour into a container, cover, and refrigerate until well chilled. Transport in a cooler. Makes 1 cup.

Curried Fish & Fruit Plates

For summery outdoor dining, cold fish salad with slices of fresh fruit is tempting fare. You can make the salad from leftover poached fish, such as red snapper, lingcod, turbot, or salmon—or use canned tuna.

- ¼ cup *each* mayonnaise and unflavored yogurt
- 2 green onions (including tops), finely chopped
- 3 tablespoons Major Grey chutney
- 1 clove garlic, minced or pressed
- ½ teaspoon curry powder
- 3 cups poached fish (see suggestions above) or 2 cans (about 7 oz. *each*) solid light tuna, drained well
  Melon slices, orange slices, grapes, and pitted and sliced plums or nectarines
- ½ cup slivered almonds, toasted

In a large bowl, combine mayonnaise, yogurt, onions, chutney (chop large pieces), garlic, and curry.

Cut fish into bite-size chunks and stir into dressing. Cover and refrigerate until well chilled. Pack fish salad, fruit, and almonds in separate containers, and transport in a cooler.

To serve, mound fish salad on individual plates, sprinkle with almonds, and surround with fruit. Makes 4 servings.

Bean & Tuna Salad

Easy, economical, and popular with picnickers of all ages, this main-dish salad can be made ahead and chilled until picnic time.

- 1 pound small or large white beans
- 1 medium-size onion, sliced
- 2 whole cloves
- 2 cans (7 oz. *each*) solid light tuna, drained well
- 1 cup olive oil
- ¼ cup red wine vinegar
- 2 cloves garlic, minced or pressed
- ½ cup chopped parsley
- 1 tablespoon capers
- 1 teaspoon salt
  Pepper

In a 3 to 4-quart pan, place beans and cover with water; let soak until next day. Drain beans and replace water; add onion and cloves. Bring to a boil over high heat; cover, reduce heat, and simmer until beans are tender (about 1¼ hours). Drain.

Meanwhile, in a large bowl, stir together tuna, oil, vinegar, garlic, parsley, capers, salt, and a dash of pepper. Add hot drained beans to tuna mixture and stir gently

Romantic Picnic for Two

A secluded, sun-dappled spot and a bottle of chilled champagne set the mood for a glorious meal à deux. And what's more fitting than food that's light, elegant, and poetically pretty: Poached Salmon Steaks with Asparagus (page 53) and Green Butter Mayonnaise, croissants with butter curls, and dainty Fresh Raspberry Barquettes (page 84).

... Bean & Tuna Salad (cont'd.)

until well blended. Cover and refrigerate until well chilled. Transport in a cooler. Makes 6 servings.

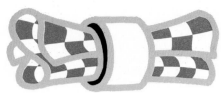

French-style Picnic Pie

With its crisp, golden crust and well-seasoned ground meat filling, this picnic pie is similar to a French *pâté en croûte.* Cut it into thick wedges, and serve it warm.

    2 tablespoons butter or
      margarine
    1 medium-size onion, chopped
    2 cloves garlic, minced or
      pressed
    ½ cup dry white wine
    1 pound ground turkey, ground
      veal, or very lean ground
      beef
    ½ pound ham, ground
    ½ cup soft bread crumbs
    ¼ cup chopped parsley
    1 egg
    ½ teaspoon *each* salt, thyme
      leaves, and dry mustard
    ¼ teaspoon ground allspice
    ⅛ teaspoon white pepper
      Egg Pastry (recipe follows)
    1 egg white beaten with 1
      teaspoon water

In a wide frying pan over medium heat, melt butter; add onion and cook until limp. Stir in garlic and wine. Bring to a boil over high heat and cook, stirring, until most of the liquid has evaporated. Transfer onion mixture to a large bowl, and stir in turkey, ham, bread crumbs, parsley, egg, salt, thyme, mustard, allspice, and pepper.

Prepare Egg Pastry. On a lightly floured board, roll larger portion into about a 12-inch circle. Fit into an 8-inch round cake pan (at least 1½ inches deep) with removable bottom. Trim pastry so it overhangs about ½ inch.

Spoon meat mixture evenly into crust. Roll remaining pastry into about a 10-inch circle and place over filling. Moisten edges; then fold top pastry under edge of bottom pastry and flute to seal. With a knife, cut a small slit in center of top crust. If desired, roll out any remaining pastry scraps, cut into decorative shapes, and arrange on crust. Brush pie evenly with egg white mixture.

Place pie on a rimmed baking sheet. Bake on lowest rack in a 375° oven for 1 hour or until well browned. Let cool for at least 15 minutes; then wrap and transport as directed on page 90. Serve warm, removing pan sides and cutting pie into wedges. Makes 6 servings.

Egg Pastry. In a bowl, combine 2 cups **all-purpose flour** and ½ teaspoon **salt.** With a pastry blender or 2 knives, cut 4 tablespoons *each* **butter** or margarine and solid **shortening** into flour mixture until it resembles coarse crumbs.

In a measuring cup, beat 1 **egg yolk;** add cold **water** to make ⅓ cup *total;* beat well. Gradually stir egg yolk mixture into flour mixture until blended. Use your hands to shape pastry into 2 balls, one a little larger than the other.

Vegetable Herb Pie

(Pictured on page 42)

Laced with cheese, bacon, and herbs, this savory vegetable

pie is a perfect candidate for a picnic: it needs little accompaniment to become a complete meal, it cuts into firm slices, and it's best when served barely warm or at room temperature.

    ½ cup uncooked rice
      About ¾ pound *each* zucchini
      and Swiss chard
    2 cups fresh or frozen peas
    ½ cup *total* finely chopped
      parsley, chopped green
      pepper, and sliced green
      onions (including tops)
    1 small onion, finely chopped
    3 cloves garlic, minced or
      pressed
    1½ cups (6 oz.) shredded Swiss
      cheese
    1 egg, lightly beaten
    2 tablespoons olive oil or salad
      oil
    1 teaspoon savory leaves
    ½ teaspoon *each* salt, pepper,
      and thyme leaves
    ½ pound sliced bacon, cut into
      1-inch pieces
      Pastry Dough (recipe follows)
    1 egg yolk beaten with 1
      tablespoon water

Place rice in a bowl and add warm water to cover; set aside. Finely chop zucchini to make 2 cups. Remove and discard white stalks from chard; chop leaves to make 2 cups.

In a large bowl, stir together zucchini, chard, peas, parsley, green pepper, green onions, onion, garlic, cheese, egg, oil, savory, salt, pepper, and thyme.

In a small frying pan over medium heat, cook bacon, stirring occasionally, until lightly browned; remove and drain on paper towels. Add to vegetable mixture. Drain rice in a wire strainer and stir into vegetable mixture.

Prepare Pastry Dough. Form into 2 equal balls. Place a ball between 2 pieces of lightly floured wax paper, and roll into about a 14-inch circle. Fit pastry into a 10-inch pie pan or quiche pan, leaving at least 1 inch hanging over edge of pan. Fill crust with vegetable mixture.

Roll out remaining dough into a ⅛-inch-thick circle and place over filling. Trim pastry, leaving a 1-inch overhang. Moisten pastry edges with egg yolk mixture, pinch to seal, and flute, if desired.

Brush pie crust with egg yolk mixture. Roll out any remaining pastry scraps, cut into decorative shapes, and arrange on crust; brush again with egg yolk mixture. With a knife, cut small slits in crust.

Bake in a 400° oven for about 1 hour; if crust begins to darken excessively, cover loosely with foil during last 15 minutes. Let cool briefly on a rack.

To serve warm, wrap and transport as directed on page 90. To serve at room temperature, cover loosely and refrigerate until well chilled; transport in a cooler, removing pie from cooler 30 minutes before serving. Makes 6 servings.

Pastry Dough. In a small pan over low heat, melt ½ cup (¼ lb.) plus 5 tablespoons **butter** or margarine. Remove from heat and stir in ⅓ cup cold **water** and 2½ cups **all-purpose flour.** Mix just until blended.

German Vegetable Pie

(Pictured on page 86)

Under its flaky, golden top crust, this wholesome pie is filled with layers of Swiss cheese, eggs, and various vegetables. It makes an excellent meatless main dish and is especially tempting when served with a piquant sour cream-Dijon mustard topping.

Pastry Dough (see above)
2 tablespoons butter or margarine
1 small onion, chopped
½ pound mushrooms, sliced
1 large Golden Delicious apple, peeled, cored, and chopped
1 tablespoon all-purpose flour
2 tablespoons Dijon mustard
¾ teaspoon dill seeds
1 can (1 lb.) sauerkraut, rinsed and excess liquid squeezed out
3 cups (12 oz.) shredded Swiss cheese
1 cup lightly packed fresh spinach leaves, rinsed and patted dry
4 hard-cooked eggs, sliced
1 egg yolk beaten with 1 tablespoon water
½ pint (1 cup) sour cream mixed with 2 tablespoons Dijon mustard (optional)

Prepare Pastry Dough. Form into 2 equal balls. Place a ball between 2 pieces of lightly floured wax paper and roll into about a 14-inch circle. Fit pastry into a 10-inch pie pan or quiche pan, leaving at least 1 inch hanging over edge of pan. Set aside.

In a wide frying pan over medium heat, melt butter; add onion and cook until limp. Stir in mushrooms and apple and cook until apple is soft. Stir in flour, mustard, and dill seeds; then mix in sauerkraut. Remove from heat.

Spread 1 cup of the cheese in bottom of pie shell. Layer with spinach, half the sauerkraut mixture, another cup of the cheese, remaining sauerkraut mixture, egg slices, and remaining cheese.

Roll out remaining dough into a ⅛-inch-thick circle and place over filling. Trim pastry, leaving a 1-inch overhang. Moisten pastry edges with egg yolk mixture, pinch to seal, and flute, if desired. (At this point you may cover lightly and chill for up to 4 hours before baking; also cover and chill remaining

egg yolk mixture and pastry scraps.)

Brush pie crust with egg yolk mixture. Roll out any remaining pastry scraps, cut into decorative shapes, and arrange on crust; brush again with egg yolk mixture. With a knife, cut small slits in crust.

Bake in a 425° oven for 15 minutes; then reduce heat to 375° and bake for 30 more minutes or until crust is golden brown. Let cool on a rack for 30 minutes; cover with foil to transport.

Serve within 2 hours, topping each wedge with sour cream-mustard mixture, if desired (take topping to picnic in a cooler). Makes 6 to 8 servings.

Crustless Ham & Cheese Pie

This creamy, flavorful union of vegetables, ham, and two kinds of cheese makes a nutritious main dish that's also easy to carry and serve. If you like, you can omit the ham and serve it as a side dish.

⅓ cup butter or margarine
¼ pound mushrooms, sliced
1 clove garlic, minced or pressed
1 medium-size zucchini, thinly sliced
1 to 1½ cups diced cooked ham
4 eggs
2 cups (1 lb.) ricotta cheese
1 cup (4 oz.) shredded jack cheese
1 package (10 oz.) frozen chopped spinach, thawed and drained well
½ teaspoon dill weed
¼ teaspoon pepper

In a wide frying pan over medium heat, melt butter; add mushrooms, garlic, and

Hearty Dutch Oven Picnic

Smoky-flavored meat filling for Barbecued Beef Sandwiches (page 43) stays hot
for several hours when it's carried in a Dutch oven wrapped in foil and several
layers of newspaper. At the picnic, spoon the meat and its thick vegetable-
laced sauce into onion rolls. Best Chocolate Chip Cookies (page 74) are a
tempting conclusion to this—or any—meal.

. . . Ham & Cheese Pie (cont'd.)

zucchini and cook just until tender when pierced (about 2 minutes). Add ham and cook for 1 more minute; set aside.

In a large bowl, beat eggs; stir in ricotta cheese, jack cheese, spinach, dill weed, pepper, and sautéed vegetables. Pour into a greased 10-inch quiche pan or pie pan.

Bake, uncovered, in a 325° oven for 35 to 40 minutes or until center is set when dish is gently shaken.

To serve hot, transport as directed on page 90. To serve at room temperature, cover loosely and refrigerate until well chilled; transport in a cooler, removing pie from cooler 30 minutes before serving. Makes 6 to 8 servings.

Tomato Tarts Niçoise

(Pictured on page 31)

The robust flavors of sunny southern France—anchovies, garlic, tomatoes, pungent Niçoise olives—mingle in these individual tarts.

Cheese Pastry (recipe follows)
¼ cup olive oil
2 large onions, slivered
1 large can (28 oz.) tomatoes
½ teaspoon each sugar and dry rosemary
⅛ teaspoon each ground red pepper (cayenne) and black pepper
2 cloves garlic, minced or pressed
2 cans (2 oz. each) flat anchovy fillets
32 Niçoise olives or medium-size ripe olives

Prepare Cheese Pastry and divide into 8 equal portions; roll each out into a circle to fit 4-inch tart pans ¾ to 1 inch deep. Line pans with pastry, trimming edges even with pan.

Heat 2 tablespoons of the oil in a large frying pan over medium heat; add onions and cook, stirring occasionally, until soft and lightly browned. Spoon onions evenly into pastry-lined pans.

In pan, heat remaining 2 tablespoons oil slightly; add tomatoes (break up with a spoon) and their liquid, sugar, rosemary, red pepper, black pepper, and garlic. Cook over high heat, stirring occasionally, until mixture is thickened and reduced to about 2 cups.

Spoon tomato mixture evenly into tart pans. Crisscross 2 anchovy fillets and arrange 4 olives on top of each tart.

Bake in a 450° oven for 20 to 25 minutes or until well browned. Let stand for about 10 minutes; then, protecting your hands, tip each tart out of its pan into your hand and place, filling side up, on a rack to cool completely. Cover and refrigerate until well chilled.

Arrange on a rimmed serving platter, cover, and transport. Makes 8 tarts.

Cheese Pastry. In a large bowl, stir together 1½ cups **all-purpose flour,** ½ teaspoon **salt,** and ¼ cup grated **Parmesan cheese.** With a pastry blender or 2 knives, cut in 4 tablespoons *each* firm **butter** or margarine and **lard** until mixture resembles coarse crumbs. With a fork, gradually stir in 2 to 3 tablespoons cold **water** until mixture begins to cling together. Use your hands to press pastry into a smooth, flat ball.

Individual Cheese Quiches

For a meatless main dish, try these attractive little cheese quiches. Baked in individual

tart pans, they can be eaten either with forks or fingers.

1½ cups all-purpose flour
¼ teaspoon salt
10 tablespoons (¼ lb. plus 2 tablespoons) butter or margarine, cut into chunks
3 eggs
1 cup (4 oz.) shredded Swiss or Gruyère cheese
1½ cups half-and-half (light cream)
Pepper
Chopped parsley

In a bowl, combine flour and salt. With a pastry blender or 2 knives, cut butter into flour mixture until it resembles fine crumbs. Add 1 of the eggs and stir with a fork until dough holds together. Shape dough into a ball. If made ahead, cover and refrigerate; bring to room temperature before continuing.

Divide dough among eight 4-inch tart pans or ten 3-inch pans. Press dough evenly over bottom and sides of pans. Place pans on a baking sheet, and evenly distribute cheese among pastry shells.

In a small bowl, beat remaining 2 eggs with half-and-half and a dash of pepper. Pour egg mixture into pastry shells (don't let mixture overflow or pastry will stick). Sprinkle with parsley.

Set baking sheet on lowest rack in a 350° oven. Bake for 35 to 40 minutes or until filling puffs and tops are lightly browned. Let stand for about 10 minutes; then, protecting your hands, tip each quiche out of its pan into your hand and place, filling side up, on a rack to cool completely. Refrigerate until well chilled.

Arrange on a rimmed serving platter, cover, and transport in a cooler. Remove from cooler 30 minutes before serving. Makes eight 4-inch quiches or ten 3-inch quiches.

Savory Sandwiches

Easy-to-serve picnic fare for any occasion

Versatile, sturdy, convenient to carry, and easy to eat, the sandwich is a neatly packaged meal in itself, a natural hub for any picnic menu—breakfast, lunch, or dinner. So many and varied are the types of sandwiches—hot and cold, open-faced and closed, delicate and hearty—that it's hard to think

of an occasion on which you wouldn't want to serve one.

In this chapter, sandwiches show up in some refreshing variations on the filling-between-two-slices-of-bread theme. You'll find such imaginative creations as sausages encased in puff pastry, and roast beef and spinach rolled up in tortillas and cut into colorful pinwheels.

Whole loaves of bread can be stuffed with savory filling and sliced to feed a crowd; or individual stuffed sandwiches

can be fashioned with pocket bread or French rolls.

As a special bonus, we take a close look at delicatessen-style meats and at some distinctive picnic breads. Using these and other ingredients, you'll be able to create sandwiches of almost unlimited diversity.

60

Dill Shrimp on Crackers

(Pictured on page 83)

Mounded on crisp English crackers, this creamy dilled shrimp mixture makes light, attractive luncheon fare.

½ pound small cooked shrimp
4 tablespoons butter or margarine
1 small clove garlic, minced or pressed
¼ teaspoon dill weed
English water crackers

Rinse shrimp and pat dry; finely chop. Using an electric mixer, beat butter until creamy; add garlic and dill. Gradually add shrimp, beating until well blended. Cover and refrigerate until well chilled or for up to 3 days. Transport in a cooler.

To serve, mound shrimp on crackers. Makes about 1⅓ cups.

Watercress-Onion Sandwiches

(Pictured on page 83)

For tea, English cooks like to serve little sandwiches like these dainty open-faced watercress and onion tidbits.

About 1 cup (½ lb.) butter or margarine, softened
½ cup chopped watercress
3 tablespoons chopped green onions (including tops)
⅛ teaspoon garlic salt
5 thin slices white bread
Watercress sprigs

In a small bowl, stir together ¾ cup of the butter, chopped watercress, onions, and garlic salt.

Just before departure, trim crusts from bread; spread each slice with butter and top with 3 tablespoons of the filling. Cut diagonally into quarters to form triangles, and top each triangle with a watercress sprig. Arrange on a serving platter and cover with plastic wrap. Transport in a cooler. Makes 20 triangles.

Pizza Focaccia Sandwiches

(Pictured on page 70)

The flat, chewy Italian bread called *focaccia* (fo-*kah*-cha) provides inspiration for this many-layered sandwich.

1 loaf (1 lb.) frozen bread dough
½ cup canned pizza sauce
⅓ cup grated Parmesan cheese
⅓ cup thinly sliced green onions (including tops)
3 tablespoons olive oil or salad oil
About ½ pound *total* thinly sliced meats (choose from dry or Toscana-style salami, coppa, galantina, mortadella)
About ½ pound thinly sliced fontina, mozzarella, provolone, or jack cheese
2 large tomatoes, thinly sliced
1 medium-size mild red or white onion, thinly sliced and separated into rings
1 can (4 oz.) whole pimentos, drained and halved, or 1 jar (9 oz.) red and yellow Italian sweet peppers, drained and halved
1 jar (6 oz.) marinated artichoke hearts

Thaw bread dough according to package directions. Pull and stretch dough to fit in bottom of a well-greased 10 by 15-inch rimmed baking sheet. With your fingers, poke holes in dough at 1-inch intervals.

Evenly spread pizza sauce over dough; then sprinkle with Parmesan cheese and green onions. Drizzle with oil. Let dough rise, uncovered, in a warm place until almost doubled (about 30 minutes).

Bake in a 450° oven for 12 to 15 minutes or until bread is well browned. Let cool; then cut into 12 pieces. Wrap in foil. (At this point, you may refrigerate bread for up to 2 days; freeze for longer storage.)

To serve, offer meats, cheese, tomatoes, onion, pimentos, and artichoke hearts to top bread. Makes 4 to 6 servings.

Chicken-Almond Fingers

(Pictured on page 83)

Toasted almonds and chopped celery add crunch to these finger-shaped chicken sandwiches. They're made on Westphalian pumpernickel bread, which lends a dense texture and nutty flavor.

1 can (5 oz.) boned chicken
2 tablespoons chopped celery
1 teaspoon Dijon mustard
3 tablespoons sour cream
¼ cup chopped toasted almonds
6 or 8 slices Westphalian pumpernickel bread
Butter or margarine, softened

Coarsely chop chicken and place in a small bowl. Add celery, mustard, sour cream, and almonds; stir until well blended. Cover and refrigerate until well chilled.

Just before departure, trim crusts from pumpernickel and cut each slice into 3 finger-shaped pieces. Spread each finger of bread with butter, top with 2 to 3 tablespoons of the chicken filling, and cover with another finger of bread. Wrap each sandwich in plastic wrap and transport in a cooler. Makes 9 or 12 sandwiches.

Grilled Bacon & Egg Sandwiches

In brisk weather, this hot and hearty combination is a good choice for an outdoor breakfast or lunch. Carry the filling and bread separately; assemble the sandwiches just before grilling over a picnic fire or campstove.

12 strips bacon, crisply cooked, drained, and crumbled

¼ cup sliced green onions (including tops)

5 hard-cooked eggs, coarsely chopped

1 cup (¼ lb.) shredded Swiss cheese

⅓ cup mayonnaise

1 tablespoon Dijon mustard

Salt and pepper

Butter or margarine

12 slices whole wheat bread

In a small container with a lid, combine bacon, onions, eggs, cheese, mayonnaise, mustard, and salt and pepper to taste; cover. (At this point, you may refrigerate until next day.) Transport in a cooler.

Just before serving, lightly butter a side of each bread slice. Spread bacon mixture on unbuttered side of 6 of the slices; top with remaining 6 slices, butter side up. In a frying pan over medium heat, grill sandwiches until golden brown on both sides. Makes 6 servings.

Bacon & Banana Sandwiches

The ever-popular standby—peanut butter and jelly—takes on a lively new dimension with the addition of crisp bacon and sliced banana.

4 slices whole wheat or firm white bread

4 tablespoons crunchy peanut butter

4 to 6 strips bacon, crisply cooked and drained

2 small bananas

1 to 2 tablespoons fruit jelly

If desired, toast bread and let cool. Evenly spread 2 slices with peanut butter; arrange bacon over top. Peel bananas and slice lengthwise; place on top of bacon. Spread your favorite fruit jelly on remaining 2 slices bread and place, jelly side down, on bananas. Makes 2 servings.

Tuna & Papaya Sandwiches

Chutney and curry season the tuna; papaya adds the accent.

8 slices whole wheat or raisin bread

1 can (6½ oz.) chunk-style tuna, drained

¼ cup mayonnaise

1 teaspoon curry powder

1½ tablespoons finely chopped Major Grey chutney

1 small papaya or 2 medium-size nectarines, halved, seeded, peeled, and sliced

If desired, toast bread and let cool. In a small bowl, combine tuna, mayonnaise, curry powder, and chutney; mix well. Spread 4 of the bread slices with tuna mixture, and cover with papaya slices. Top with remaining 4 bread slices. Transport in a cooler. Makes 4 servings.

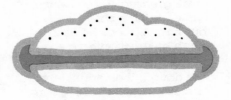

Curried Ham on Rye

You can mix and chill this versatile curried ham spread a day ahead, if you like. Assemble the sandwiches at home or take the spread and buttered slices of rye bread to the picnic for do-it-yourself open-faced sandwiches. If you prefer, you can spoon the spread onto broad slices of crisp vegetables instead.

1 small package (3 oz.) cream cheese, softened

1 tablespoon mayonnaise

½ teaspoon each curry powder and Dijon mustard

2 drops liquid hot pepper seasoning

2 tablespoons finely chopped sweet pickle

¼ cup finely diced celery

½ cup finely chopped green onions (including tops)

1½ cups (about 8 oz.) finely diced, fully cooked ham

Salt and pepper

Butter or margarine, softened

8 slices dark rye bread

In a small bowl, beat together cream cheese, mayonnaise, curry powder, mustard, and hot pepper seasoning until smooth. Stir in pickle, celery, green onions, and ham; mix well. Season to taste with salt and pepper. Cover and refrigerate for at least an hour or until next day. Transport in a cooler.

To prepare sandwiches, lightly butter a side of each bread slice; evenly spread ham mixture over buttered side of 4 slices and top with remaining 4 slices, butter side down. (Or put buttered bread slices together and carry along with ham mixture; then assemble open-faced sandwiches just before eating.) Wrap sandwiches or bread airtight. Makes 4 servings.

Fiesta by the Pool

Thin slices of marinated, grilled flank steak are topped with cilantro-flavored tomato and avocado salsa, then rolled in warm tortillas to make Barbecued Mexican Sandwiches (page 66). For a perfect summertime repast, serve them with a big pitcher of thirst-quenching Chilled Citrus Sangría (page 80) and butter lettuce salad garnished with orange slices, ripe olives, and red onion rings.

International Breads: A Baker's Dozen

Where picnics are concerned, bread is indeed the staff of life—its uses in *alfresco* dining are almost unlimited. For something a little out of the ordinary, consider the following breads from all over the world. And remember always to look for absolute freshness.

Bagels. Nothing beats a good bagel! Glossy and doughnut-shaped, firm and chewy, these traditional Jewish rolls are available in the standard plain version, or covered with poppy seeds, sesame seeds, bits of onion, or coarse kosher salt. They come in whole wheat and pumpernickel variations, and sometimes in miniature "cocktail" size.

Baguettes. Visit a deli or bakery for these long, skinny loaves of crusty French bread so dear to Parisian hearts. Try tearing a baguette into chunks or slicing thin diagonals to be served with cheese; or split one lengthwise, spread with your favorite filling, and slice to make sandwiches.

Boston brown bread. This moist dark bread contains molasses, raisins, and nuts, and has a tender, cakelike texture. It's sold in cans, so at the picnic you can just open a can, slide the bread out, and slice it into thick rounds.

Brioches. Buttery and rich, yet wonderfully airy, brioches are top-knotted French yeast rolls that come in several sizes and are delicious with pâté and cheese. Or slice off their tops and hollow out the centers; when you get to the picnic site, fill with cold meat or seafood salad.

Croissants. Croissants are flaky French crescent rolls. They're traditionally served with butter and preserves for breakfast, but there's no reason for them not to leave the breakfast table and travel outdoors. They make a distinctive picnic bread served with soups or salads.

Focaccia. Bakers in Genoa, Italy, invented this flat, chewy bread that resembles thick, seasoned pizza crust. It can be flavored with such ingredients as sage, olives, tomato sauce, onion, or raisins.

Italian bread sticks. These come in various lengths and may be studded with seasonings such as coarse salt, poppy seeds, fennel seeds, or sesame seeds.

Lahvosh. A flat Armenian cracker bread, lahvosh has a nutty taste that comes from sesame seeds. Traditionally, it's sold in enormous rounds that you break into serving-size portions. For convenience on a picnic, though, you may want the smaller, cracker-size version.

Onion rolls. Tender, golden rolls, flecked with moist morsels of onion, are a lively alternative to other breads for sandwich-making. Their zesty flavor goes well with hearty sandwich fillings—especially pastrami, corned beef, and smoked ham.

Pita. Also known as Armenian or Arab pocket bread, pita is used in the Middle East to enclose various savory stuffings. To use, cut or tear each circle in half, pull the pocket open, and insert filling.

Scandinavian flatbread. There are many versions of flatbread in Scandinavian cuisine, but perhaps the best known is Swedish cracker bread. It comes both in large wheels and shaped like ordinary crackers.

Tortillas. Versatile is the word for these flat, unleavened rounds of Mexican bread. Select either the small, coarse-textured corn tortillas or the more delicate white or whole wheat flour ones. Spread them with any filling, and roll or fold them up.

Westphalian pumpernickel. Darker and denser than what we usually think of as pumpernickel, this German bread comes in small, thin squares and is coarse-textured, chewy, and slightly sweet.

Barbecued Lamb in Pocket Bread

(Pictured on page 7)

Skewers of spicy lamb cubes cook quickly on a barbecue or hibachi. Combine them with vegetables and yogurt in warm pocket bread for a satisfying, whole-meal sandwich.

You can barbecue the meat at the site just before serving, or cook it at home and take it to the picnic, wrapped to keep warm.

½ cup lemon juice
¼ cup olive oil or salad oil
1 teaspoon *each* chopped fresh coriander (cilantro) and ground cumin
½ teaspoon *each* black pepper and turmeric
¼ teaspoon crushed red pepper
2 pounds lean boneless lamb (shoulder or leg), cut into ¾-inch cubes
2 large onions, thinly sliced and separated into rings
6 pocket breads
½ pint (1 cup) unflavored yogurt
2 tablespoons *each* chopped fresh mint and cucumber
12 to 24 small romaine spears
3 medium-size tomatoes, cut into thin wedges
2 medium-size cucumbers, thinly sliced (optional)
Chutney (optional)

Combine lemon juice, oil, coriander, cumin, black pepper, turmeric, and red pepper. Place lamb and onions in separate containers with lids; pour half the marinade over meat; pour remaining half over onions. Cover and refrigerate for about 3 hours. Transport in a cooler.

Lift meat from marinade and drain briefly, reserving marinade. Thread meat on sturdy metal skewers. Place on a lightly greased grill 4 to 6 inches above a solid bed of glowing coals. Cook, turning and basting frequently with reserved marinade, for 12 to 15 minutes or until lamb is well browned on all sides but still pink in center when slashed.

Meanwhile, stack pocket breads on a sheet of heavy foil. Wrap tightly and place at edge of grill to warm for about 10 minutes; turn over several times to heat evenly. In a small bowl, combine yogurt, mint, and cucumber.

To serve, drain onion and tear or cut pocket breads in half. In each half put 1 or 2 romaine spears, 5 or 6 lamb cubes, some onion rings, tomato wedges, cucumber slices and chutney, if desired, and a dollop of yogurt mixture. Makes 6 to 12 servings.

Mediterranean Salad Sandwich

Halves of chewy pocket bread form just the right hollows for this crunchy tuna salad. Carry the salad and dressing separately, ready to combine and enclose in the bread when you stop for lunch.

1 jar (6 oz.) marinated artichoke hearts
1 can (6½ oz.) chunk-style tuna, drained and broken into pieces
2 cups shredded iceberg lettuce
½ mild red onion, thinly sliced and separated into rings
1 can (2¼ oz.) sliced ripe olives, drained
½ small cucumber, thinly sliced
6 radishes, sliced
2 tablespoons lemon juice
¼ teaspoon *each* dry basil and oregano leaves
Salt and pepper
4 pocket breads

Drain artichoke hearts, reserving marinade. In a 2-quart container with a lid, combine artichoke hearts, tuna, lettuce, onion rings, olives, cucumber, and radishes. Cover and refrigerate until time to leave. Transport in a cooler.

Combine reserved artichoke marinade, lemon juice, basil, and oregano; pour into a container. Cover and let stand at room temperature.

To serve, pour dressing over tuna salad and mix well; season to taste with salt and pepper. Tear or cut breads in half; evenly spoon salad mixture into pockets. Makes 8 servings.

Vegetable Pockets

This crisp raw vegetable salad goes together quickly from ingredients generally on hand, so it's an ideal choice for spur-of-the-moment sandwiches.

If you prefer, use purchased taco shells or soft flour tortillas instead of pocket bread to hold the filling.

4 cups finely shredded cabbage or lettuce
2 green onions (including tops), thinly sliced
1 stalk celery, thinly sliced
1 large carrot, thinly sliced
½ cup chopped green pepper, or 5 or 6 radishes, thinly sliced
1 cup (4 oz.) shredded sharp Cheddar, Swiss, or jack cheese
Salt and pepper
4 or 5 pocket breads
1 to 1½ cups creamy style salad dressing (such as green goddess or thousand island), homemade or purchased
1 can (3 oz.) French-fried onions or about ¾ cup toasted slivered almonds

In a large bowl, combine cabbage, onions, celery, carrot,

green pepper, and cheese. Season to taste with salt and pepper. Cover and refrigerate until time to leave. Transport in a cooler.

To serve, tear or cut pocket breads in half; spoon salad mixture into a bread pocket, top with dressing, and sprinkle with French-fried onions. Makes 8 to 10 servings.

Roast Beef & Spinach Pinwheels

(Pictured on page 67)

Soft flour tortillas embellished with tasty sandwich makings are rolled up jelly roll fashion and cut into individual servings to make hearty, easy-to-handle pinwheels for grandstand munching.

- 1 small package (3 oz.) cream cheese, softened
- 1 tablespoon prepared horseradish
- ¼ teaspoon pepper
  About 1 tablespoon milk
- 1 very large flour tortilla (13 to 14 inches in diameter) or 2 medium-size flour tortillas (*each* 6 to 8 inches in diameter), at room temperature
- ⅓ to ½ pound very thinly sliced roast beef
- 2 medium-size tomatoes, very thinly sliced
- 6 to 8 spinach leaves

In a small bowl, beat cream cheese until light and fluffy. Stir in horseradish, pepper, and enough milk so cheese will spread easily.

Lightly moisten both sides of tortilla with water; lay flat and spread with cheese mixture. Evenly layer beef, tomatoes, and spinach on top. Roll up. Wrap in a damp paper towel, then in plastic wrap.

Refrigerate for up to 4 hours. Transport in a cooler.

To serve, cut roll into 2 to 3-inch pieces. Makes 4 servings.

Mu Shu Burgers

This tasty ground pork sandwich is a Peking-style burrito, inspired by the flavorful ingredients of mu shu pork.

Hoisin sauce is available in Oriental markets; apple butter can be substituted, though it lacks authentic flavor.

- 1 pound lean ground pork
- 1 small onion, chopped
- ¼ cup fine dry bread crumbs
- 1 egg
- ½ cup finely chopped water chestnuts, jicama, or celery
- 1 clove garlic, minced or pressed
- 2 tablespoons soy sauce
- ½ teaspoon ground ginger
- ½ to ¾ cup hoisin sauce
- ¾ to 1 cup green onions, cut into matchstick-size pieces
  About 1 cup bean sprouts
  Fresh coriander (cilantro or Chinese parsley) sprigs (optional)
- 8 flour tortillas, 6 to 8 inches in diameter

In a bowl, combine pork, onion, crumbs, egg, water chestnuts, garlic, soy, and ginger. Shape into 8 logs, each about 3 inches long. Place hoisin sauce, green onions,

bean sprouts, and coriander in separate containers. Transport meat and condiments in a cooler.

Lightly moisten both sides of tortillas with water; stack tortillas and wrap in heavy foil.

To cook, place pork logs on a grill 4 to 6 inches above a solid bed of glowing coals. Grill, turning to brown evenly, for 12 to 14 minutes *total* or until meat in center is no longer pink when slashed. Place foil-wrapped tortillas at edge of grill; turn over often to heat evenly.

To serve, spread some hoisin on a tortilla. Place a pork log near lower edge and top with some onions, bean sprouts, and coriander. Fold edge of tortilla over filling; fold in sides and roll up to enclose meat and vegetables. Makes 8 servings.

Barbecued Mexican Sandwiches

(Pictured on page 63)

Ahead of time, you marinate the steak in a container you can carry to the picnic site, and you also prepare the salsa. At your destination, quickly cook the meat, then enclose it in warm soft flour tortillas.

- Tomato Salsa (recipe follows)
- ¼ cup *each* olive oil and white wine vinegar
- ½ teaspoon oregano leaves
- ⅛ teaspoon pepper
- 3 cloves garlic, minced or pressed
- 1 large (about 1½ lbs.) flank steak
- 12 large flour tortillas, 8 to 10 inches in diameter
- 1 firm ripe avocado

Prepare Tomato Salsa.

In a 1-cup glass measure, stir together oil, vinegar, oreg-

Grandstand Picnic

No matter what the sport, you'll bleacher-sit in style with an easily portable family picnic. Thyme-scented Carrot Soup (page 22) with jumbo croutons is delicious sipped or spooned from plastic cups, and Roast Beef & Spinach Pinwheels (page 66) add a new twist to sandwich-munching. With a supply of cookies, fruit, and drinks, you'll have ample sustenance even if the game goes into overtime.

ano, pepper, and garlic. Place steak in a close-fitting container with a lid or in a heavy plastic bag. Pour oil mixture over meat; cover and refrigerate for 6 hours or until next day. Transport in a cooler.

To cook, lift meat from marinade, drain briefly, and place on a lightly greased grill, 4 to 6 inches above a solid bed of glowing coals. Cook, turning once, for 5 to 8 minutes per side for rare or until done to your liking when slashed. Remove meat to a board and cut across the grain into thin, slanting slices.

Meanwhile, place tortillas, one at a time, directly on grill. Heat, turning once, for about 30 seconds per side or until soft and hot. Immediately stack tortillas and wrap in dampened cloth or foil to keep warm. Peel, pit, and dice avocado; gently stir into salsa.

To serve, place meat strips down center of each tortilla, top with salsa, and roll up. Makes about 6 servings.

Tomato Salsa. In a small container with a lid, combine 2 medium-size **tomatoes,** peeled, seeded, and finely chopped; 3 finely chopped **green onions** (including tops); 2 tablespoons chopped canned **green chiles;** 2 tablespoons chopped fresh **coriander** (cilantro) or ½ teaspoon ground coriander; ½ teaspoon **salt;** and 1 tablespoon **olive oil.** Cover and refrigerate for 6 hours or until next day.

Potato Pups

(Pictured on page 18)

Two all-time picnic favorites— hot dogs and potato salad— can be assembled in neat foil packets the day before your picnic, ready to heat just before you leave home.

Choose regular frankfurters and buns, or substitute other fully cooked sausages such as kielbasa, garlic frankfurters, or smoked sausage links. If you wish, you can use French rolls instead of buns.

- **¾ pound red thin-skinned potatoes**
- **4 strips bacon**
- **8 frankfurters or other fully cooked sausages**
- **¼ cup thinly sliced green onions (including tops)**
- **2 hard-cooked eggs, chopped**
- **½ cup mayonnaise**
- **3 to 4 tablespoons prepared mustard**
- **2 tablespoons sweet pickle relish, drained**
- **Salt and pepper**
- **8 frankfurter buns or French rolls**

Pour water into a 2 to 3-quart pan to a depth of about 1 inch. Bring to a boil over high heat; add potatoes. Cover, reduce heat, and cook until tender when pierced (20 to 30 minutes). Drain and let cool; peel, if desired, and cut into ½-inch cubes.

In a wide frying pan over medium heat, cook bacon until crisp; lift out, drain, and crumble. Discard all but 2 tablespoons drippings. Cut frankfurters almost through, lengthwise; spread open and place in pan. Cook over medium heat, turning as needed, until lightly browned on both sides; set aside.

In a medium-size bowl, combine potatoes, bacon, onions, and eggs. In a cup, stir together mayonnaise, 2 tablespoons of the mustard, and pickle relish. Stir into potato mixture and season to taste with salt and pepper.

To assemble, place a frankfurter, cut side up, in each bun; spread each evenly with some of the remaining mustard, and

evenly spoon over potato mixture. Wrap separately in foil and twist ends to seal. (At this point, you may refrigerate packets until next day.)

Heat foil-wrapped buns in a 350° oven for about 15 minutes or until heated through.

Transport as directed on page 90. Serve within 2 hours. Makes 8 servings.

Pastry-wrapped Sausages

(Pictured on page 10)

When baked, thinly rolled puff pastry filled with cooked sausage links comes out of the oven as puffy little pillows.

- **1 package (10 oz.) frozen patty shells**
- **12 pork sausage links, cooked, cooled, and split almost through, lengthwise**

Thaw patty shells. Roll each out on a lightly floured board into a rectangle about 3½ by 8 inches; cut in half to make two 3½ by 4-inch pieces. Top each with a sausage link, cut side down. Fold pastry over sausage, moisten edges with water, and press together with a fork to seal along length of sausage, leaving link ends exposed.

Place on ungreased rimmed baking sheets. Prick tops with a fork and bake in a 400° oven for 25 minutes or until richly browned. To serve hot, transport as directed on page 90. Or let cool and transport in a picnic basket.

If made ahead, let cool, wrap airtight, and freeze. To reheat, bake frozen pastries, uncovered, in a 400° oven for about 8 minutes or until heated through. Makes 4 to 6 servings.

Deli Meats Add Easy Variety

Cold cuts from a well-stocked delicatessen adapt to almost any picnic situation. What could be more elegant than a paper-thin slice of prosciutto wrapped around a crescent of fresh melon, or more casual than a dry salami and a chunk of cheese carried in a backpack on a hike? You can serve deli meats alone, with crackers or fruit, or as fixings for spur-of-the-moment sandwiches.

Shopping for deli meats can be fun, too, if you taste before you buy, ask questions, and aren't afraid to venture into unfamiliar territory. Remember, though, that most of these meats must be kept cool to avoid spoilage, so don't buy them for an all-day, hot-weather picnic unless you have some form of refrigeration.

Beef. For sandwiches, try thinly sliced *roast beef*, *corned beef* (cured in brine), and *pastrami* (peppered and smoked).

Beerwurst. This German sausage, usually made from ground veal and pork with chunky pieces of ham, is sometimes spelled *bierwurst*.

Blutwurst. You'll recognize blutwurst, or blood sausage, by its deep maroon color. It's made from pig's blood, chopped lean pork, and pork fat; chunks of pork tongue are often added as well.

Bologna. Usually made from beef, pork, and veal, bologna is commonly available in several forms: *German bologna* is spiced with garlic; *Vienna bologna* contains pistachios; and *Lebanon bologna* is a heavily smoked, all-beef bologna from Lebanon, Pennsylvania.

Coppa. Pork shoulder butt is rolled and peppered with red or black pepper, and then cured. It can be mild or spicy. When it's cooked rather than dry-cured, it's called *capocolla*. A layer of salami wrapped around a core of coppa constitutes *coppa veneziana*.

Galantina. An Italian pork and veal loaf is flavored with pistachios and pork fat to make galantina.

Ham. Look for *Westphalian ham* (strong, juniper-smoked German ham), *Black Forest ham* (less heavily smoked), and plain *smoked ham* (milder still). Also try *prosciutto*, the tender, dry-cured Italian ham that is traditionally sliced paper-thin and wrapped around bread sticks or melon wedges.

Head cheese (sulze). This mixture of meats from the head or other parts of a pig or calf is suspended in gelatin. *French-style head cheese* contains additional vinegar and spices, and has a tangier flavor.

Liverwurst. There's great variation in the taste and texture of liverwurst. Some common examples are *braunschweiger* (smoked and heavily seasoned, soft and easy to spread), *country-style liverwurst* (also boasts a lot of seasoning and may contain pieces of bacon fat), and *Bavarian liverwurst* (studded with pistachios).

Mortadella. This subtly seasoned bologna is usually made of pork, veal, and beef; it's flavored with garlic, peppercorns, and sometimes pistachio nuts.

Salami. This heavily seasoned Italian sausage of pork, and sometimes beef, is usually dried, but sometimes cooked. When cooked it appears fuller and moister and is called *salami cotto*. You can choose *Italian dry salami*, *Toscano salami* (cured in wine), all-beef *kosher salami*, or the somewhat milder *Genoa salami* or *German salami*.

Thuringer. A pronounced smoky flavor is characteristic of this German summer sausage; it has a smoother, leaner texture than salami.

Turkey. Don't overlook this outstanding sandwich component. For additional flavor, try smoked turkey.

Zampino. Deli-style zampino is a mild-flavored meat made from salami cotto wrapped in pork rind.

Alfresco Italian Lunch

Feature build-your-own Pizza Focaccia Sandwiches (page 61) for an informal Italian luncheon. You start with flat, pizza-like bread and pile on your choice of sandwich toppings—here, we used salami, galantina, provolone cheese, onion, tomato, Italian sweet peppers, and marinated artichoke hearts. What to drink? Chianti and Italian mineral water, of course. The nutty Crumb Cooky (page 73) is baked in one piece, then broken into chunks to serve with melon wedges, figs, and espresso.

Savory Sandwich Loaf

When you're on the go—horseback riding, bicycling, or hiking—you want a hearty yet sturdy sandwich. One meal that travels well is this French loaf stuffed with savory ham and chicken.

1 long loaf (1 lb.) French bread
2 cups (about 8 oz.) very finely chopped cooked chicken or turkey
2 cups (about 8 oz.) finely chopped cooked ham
4 hard-cooked eggs, chopped
⅓ cup finely chopped green onions (including tops)
1 cup finely chopped dill pickles, drained
½ cup chopped parsley
Caper-Mustard Dressing (recipe follows)
Garlic salt and pepper

Cut a 1½-inch-thick slice off each end of bread; set aside. With a long serrated knife, cut and pull out soft center (save for other uses), leaving a shell about ½ inch thick; set aside.

In a bowl, combine chicken, ham, eggs, onions, pickles, and parsley. Prepare Caper-Mustard Dressing and stir into chicken mixture. Season to taste with garlic salt and pepper.

Stand hollow loaf on end and stuff with filling, using a long-handled wooden spoon to pack tightly. Set end slices in place; wrap in foil and refrigerate for at least 4 hours or until next day. Unwrap and cut into ¾-inch slices. Rewrap loaf in foil and refrigerate until time to leave. Transport in a cooler. Makes 4 to 6 servings.

Caper-Mustard Dressing.
In a small bowl, blend 6 tablespoons **mayonnaise** with 3 tablespoons drained **capers**, 2 tablespoons Dijon **mustard**, 2 teaspoons *each* **vinegar** and **Worcestershire**, and 1 teaspoon **thyme leaves.**

Spanish Omelet Picnic Loaf

(Pictured on front cover)

This version of a Spanish-style omelet nestles inside a big round loaf of French bread.

1 large round loaf French bread, 10 to 12 inches in diameter
About 4 tablespoons olive oil
About 10 ounces chorizo or linguica sausage
1 large thin-skinned potato, cooked
1 medium-size onion, finely chopped
1 clove garlic, minced or pressed
1 medium-size green pepper, chopped
1 medium-size red bell pepper, chopped, or 1 jar (4 oz.) pimentos, drained and chopped
9 eggs
¾ teaspoon salt
¼ teaspoon pepper

With a serrated knife, split bread in half horizontally. Pull out soft center (save for other uses) from each half, leaving a 1-inch shell. Brush cut surfaces of shells with about 1 tablespoon of the oil. Reassemble loaf, wrap in foil, and place in a 300° oven while preparing omelet.

In a 10-inch nonstick omelet or frying pan over medium heat, crumble chorizo (discard casing) and cook until lightly browned. With a slotted spoon, remove sausage, drain, and set aside. Discard drippings.

Peel and thinly slice potato. Heat 1 tablespoon of the oil in pan over medium-high heat; add potato, onion, and garlic. Cook, turning often, until potato is browned (about 3 minutes). Add green and red peppers and cook for 1 minute. Stir in sausage; then remove pan from heat.

Break eggs into a bowl, add salt and pepper, and beat with a fork. Place pan over medium heat; push potato mixture to one side and add 1 more tablespoon of the oil to pan. Redistribute vegetables in pan and pour in eggs. As edges begin to set, push toward center and shake pan vigorously to allow uncooked egg to flow underneath.

Cook omelet until top is just set but appears moist, and bottom is lightly browned (about 5 minutes). To loosen omelet, run a wide spatula around edge and underneath. Invert a plate over pan and, with one hand on plate, quickly invert pan, turning omelet out onto plate. Add remaining 1 tablespoon oil to pan, gently slide omelet back into pan, and cook over medium heat until bottom is lightly browned (about 2 minutes); remove pan from heat.

Remove bread from oven; invert bottom half of bread over omelet and, with one hand on bread, quickly invert pan, turning omelet out onto loaf. Place top of bread over omelet. Transport as directed on page 90.

If made ahead, refrigerate wrapped loaf until next day. Before leaving, reheat in a 400° oven for 25 to 30 minutes or until omelet is hot and steamy. Makes about 6 servings.

Sweet Conclusions

Desserts to finish the feast with a flourish

Fresh air means hearty appetites, so no matter how bountiful a banquet you're serving, you'll probably want to include a special treat at the meal's end. Picnic desserts can be as simple or as elaborate as you like—the only requirement is that they be portable, easy to serve, and fun to eat outdoors.

Sturdy drop cookies and bar cookies that can travel in their baking pans are good picnic choices. So are cupcakes and individual tarts, if you want easy-to-eat cake or pie. But don't rule out more complicated confections. Family-size cakes can work beautifully away from home, especially those that are single-layered and moist enough to go unfrosted. This is true for pies and tarts, too, if their crusts aren't too fragile and the fillings are firm.

Ripe, fresh fruit is lovely by itself, or you can enhance it with a sauce, dip, or marinade. And if you really want to provide a flourish, present an elegant dessert fondue.

Crumb Cooky

(Pictured on page 70)

In Italy, this oversize nut cooky is known as *torta fregolotti*. Bake it ahead of time, then break it into chunks to serve.

    1 cup blanched or unblanched
       almonds
    2⅔ cups all-purpose flour
    1 cup sugar
       Pinch of salt
    1 teaspoon grated lemon peel
    1 cup (½ lb.) plus 2 tablespoons
       butter or margarine, softened
    2 tablespoons lemon juice
    1 tablespoon brandy or water

In a blender or food processor, whirl almonds until finely ground. In a bowl, combine ground almonds, flour, sugar, salt, and lemon peel. With a pastry blender or 2 knives, cut butter into flour mixture until it resembles coarse crumbs. Sprinkle with lemon juice and brandy and mix lightly with a fork until blended.

Spread mixture (it should be crumbly) in a greased and floured 12-inch pizza pan (do not press into pan). Bake in a 350° oven for 50 to 60 minutes or until browned. Let cool on a rack.

When thoroughly cooled, wrap well and let stand for at least a day. To serve, break into chunks. Makes 2 to 3 dozen pieces.

Walnut Jewel Cookies

(Pictured on page 7)

Little "gems" of red currant jelly sparkle in the centers of these plump, nutty cookies.

    1 cup (½ lb.) butter or
       margarine, softened
    ½ cup firmly packed light brown
       sugar
    2 egg yolks
    ½ teaspoon vanilla
    2½ cups all-purpose flour
    ¼ teaspoon salt
    1 egg white, lightly beaten
    1½ cups finely chopped walnuts
    3 to 4 tablespoons red currant
       jelly

In a large bowl, cream butter and brown sugar until fluffy. Beat in egg yolks and vanilla until well blended. In another bowl, combine flour and salt; gradually add flour mixture to creamed mixture, beating until well blended.

For each cooky, roll dough into a ball about 1 inch in diameter, and dip into egg white. Roll in chopped nuts. Place balls about 1 inch apart on greased baking sheets.

With your thumb or the tip of a spoon, make a depression in center of each cooky, and fill each with about ¼ teaspoon of the jelly. Bake in a 375° oven for 12 to 15 minutes or until lightly browned. Transfer to racks and let cool. Makes about 3½ dozen cookies.

Buttery Lemon Squares

These rich, lemony treats are a first-class finish for an outdoor meal. For easy handling, carry them in their baking pan.

    1 cup (½ lb.) butter or margarine
    ½ cup powdered sugar
    2⅓ cups all-purpose flour
    4 eggs
    2 cups granulated sugar
    1 teaspoon grated lemon peel
    6 tablespoons lemon juice
    1 teaspoon baking powder
    3 tablespoons powdered sugar

In a large bowl, cream butter and the ½ cup powdered sugar until light and fluffy. Add 2 cups of the flour and beat until blended. Spread evenly in a well-greased 9 by 13-inch baking pan. Bake in a 350° oven for 20 minutes.

Meanwhile, in a small bowl, beat eggs until light and frothy. Gradually add granulated sugar, beating until thickened and well blended. Add lemon peel, lemon juice, remaining ⅓ cup flour, and baking powder; beat until thoroughly blended. Pour lemon mixture over baked crust, return to oven and bake for 15 to 20 more minutes or until pale gold.

Remove from oven and sprinkle evenly with the 3 tablespoons powdered sugar; let cool. To serve, cut into small squares. Makes about 20 squares.

Guatemalan Sugar Cookies

(Pictured on page 23)

When your menu features south-of-the-border dishes, offer these chocolate-sprinkled sugar cookies based on a traditional Latin-American recipe.

    ½ cup (¼ lb.) butter or
       margarine, softened
    ½ cup lard
    ¾ cup sugar
    1 egg yolk
    1 teaspoon *each* vanilla and
       grated orange rind
    2½ cups all-purpose flour
    ½ teaspoon ground cinnamon
       Dash of salt
       Sugar
       Chocolate sprinkles

In a large bowl, cream butter, lard, and the ¾ cup sugar until fluffy. Beat in egg yolk, vanilla, and orange rind. In another bowl, combine flour, cinnamon, and salt; gradually add flour mixture to creamed mixture, beating until well blended.

Sprinkle sugar on a piece of wax paper. For each cooky, roll dough into a ball the size of a small walnut, and roll in sugar until completely coated. Place balls about 2 inches apart on greased baking sheets. Grease bottom of a glass, dip in sugar, and press each cooky down to about ½-inch thickness. Sprinkle centers lightly with chocolate sprinkles.

Bake in a 275° oven for 20 minutes; then raise temperature to 350° and bake for 8 to 10 more minutes or until lightly browned. Carefully transfer to racks (hot cookies are delicate) and let cool. Makes about 3 dozen cookies.

Cut-out Sugar Cookies

(Pictured on page 18)

Use cardboard cooky patterns that you make yourself to create crisp, buttery sugar cookies in any shape you like. Or you can use commercial cooky cutters instead.

¾ cup (¼ lb. plus 4 tablespoons) butter or margarine, softened

1 cup sugar

2 eggs

1 teaspoon vanilla

1 teaspoon *each* baking powder and salt

About 3 cups all-purpose flour

To make cooky patterns, trace or draw large (about 3 by 5 inches) block numbers, letters, or other shapes on sturdy cardboard (about 1/16 inch thick). Cut with scissors, making smooth edges.

In a large bowl, cream butter and sugar until light and fluffy. Beat in eggs and vanilla. In another bowl, combine baking powder, salt, and 2¾ cups of the flour; add flour mixture to creamed mixture, stirring to form a soft dough. (At this point, you may cover and refrigerate for up to 3 days. Let dough come to room temperature before continuing.)

Divide dough into 12 equal portions. On a lightly floured board, roll each portion ⅛ inch thick. Place cardboard pattern on top of dough and cut around edge; lift off excess dough and set aside (roll scraps again for additional cookies). Transfer cookies to ungreased baking sheets.

Bake in a 400° oven for 8 to 10 minutes or until edges begin to brown. Transfer immediately to racks and let cool completely. Store in an airtight container. Makes about 2 dozen cookies.

Cheesecake Cookies

(Pictured on page 39)

These cookies have all the rich creaminess of cheesecake and all the convenience of an easy-to-serve bar cooky. To make enough for a crowd, double the ingredients and use a 9 by 13-inch baking pan.

⅓ cup butter or margarine

⅓ cup firmly packed brown sugar

1 cup all-purpose flour

½ cup finely chopped walnuts

¼ cup granulated sugar

1 large package (8 oz.) cream cheese

1 egg

½ teaspoon vanilla

2 tablespoons milk

1 tablespoon lemon juice

In a small bowl, cream butter and brown sugar until light and fluffy. With a fork, blend in flour until mixture resembles fine crumbs. Stir in walnuts. Reserving 1 cup for topping, press remaining mixture into a greased 8-inch square pan. Bake in a 350° oven for 12 to 15 minutes.

Meanwhile, in another bowl, beat granulated sugar and cream cheese together until fluffy. Add egg, vanilla, milk, and lemon juice; beat until smooth. Pour cream cheese mixture over baked crust, and sprinkle evenly with remaining crumb mixture.

Bake in a 350° oven for 20 minutes. Let cool; then refrigerate. Transport in pan, packed in a cooler. To serve, cut into squares and remove from pan with a spatula. Makes 16 cookies.

Best Chocolate Chip Cookies

(Pictured on page 58)

Everyone likes chocolate chip cookies, but aficionados will want to try this lavish version. It's truly an extravaganza.

1 cup solid shortening

½ cup (¼ lb.) butter or margarine

1⅓ cups granulated sugar

1 cup firmly packed brown sugar

4 eggs

1 tablespoon vanilla

1 teaspoon lemon juice

2 teaspoons baking soda

1½ teaspoons salt

1 teaspoon ground cinnamon

½ cup regular or quick-cooking rolled oats

3 cups all-purpose flour

2 large packages (12 oz. *each*) semisweet chocolate chips

2 cups chopped walnuts

(Continued on page 76)

Chocolate Fondue Finale

Following a picnic meal or simply on its own, Picnic Chocolate Fondue
(page 79) is an elegant outdoor dessert. To dip in rich, glossy hot chocolate
sauce, we offer chunks of apple, wedges of kiwi fruit, cubes of pound cake,
and succulent strawberries and raspberries; you can substitute other fruits,
plain cakes, or soft cookies such as macaroons. Pour the cognac . . . and
enjoy.

In a large bowl, place shortening, butter, granulated sugar, and brown sugar. Using an electric mixer on high speed, cream until light and fluffy (about 5 minutes). Add eggs, one at a time, beating well after each addition. Beat in vanilla and lemon juice.

In another bowl, stir together baking soda, salt, cinnamon, oats, and flour. Beat flour mixture into butter mixture until well blended; stir in chocolate chips and nuts.

For each cooky, drop a scant ¼ cup dough on a lightly greased baking sheet; space cookies about 3 inches apart. Bake in a 350° oven for 16 to 18 minutes or until golden brown. Transfer cookies to racks to cool. Makes about 3 dozen large cookies.

Ginger Oatmeal Cookies

Sturdy enough to travel in a backpack or bike basket, these chewy, crisp cookies are also easy to make.

    ¾ cup (¼ lb. plus 4 tablespoons) butter or margarine
    1 cup sugar
    1 egg
    ¼ cup light molasses
    1½ cups all-purpose flour
    2 teaspoons baking soda
    ½ teaspoon salt
    1 teaspoon ground cinnamon
    ¾ teaspoon *each* ground cloves and ground ginger
    2 cups regular or quick-cooking rolled oats

In a bowl, cream butter and sugar until light and fluffy. Beat in egg and molasses until smooth. In another bowl, stir together flour, baking soda, salt, cinnamon, cloves, and ginger; stir flour mixture into butter mixture until blended. Stir in oats.

For each cooky, drop a tablespoon of dough on a lightly greased baking sheet; space cookies about 3 inches apart.

Bake in a 350° oven for about 8 minutes or until browned. Let cool on baking sheets for about a minute; then transfer cookies to racks to cool completely. Makes about 4 dozen cookies.

Chunky Peanut Butter Cookies

Kids and peanut butter just seem to go together, and that's why these crunchy peanut butter cookies are sure to please at a family picnic. Made with wholesome ingredients, they are quite nutritious, and they travel well, too.

    ½ cup (¼ lb.) butter or margarine
    ¾ cup firmly packed light brown sugar
    ¼ cup honey
    1 egg
    ½ teaspoon vanilla
    1 cup crunchy peanut butter
    1½ cups all-purpose flour
    ½ teaspoon *each* salt and baking soda
    ½ cup wheat germ

In a bowl, cream butter and brown sugar until light and fluffy. Beat in honey, egg, vanilla, and peanut butter until thoroughly blended. In another bowl, stir together flour, salt, baking soda, and wheat germ; stir flour mixture into butter mixture just until well blended.

For each cooky, roll a level tablespoon of dough into a ball, and place on a greased baking sheet; space cookies about 3 inches apart. Flatten balls with a fork dipped in flour.

Bake in a 325° oven for 15 minutes or until edges are lightly browned. Let cool on baking sheets for about a minute; then transfer cookies to racks to cool completely. Makes about 4 dozen cookies.

Filbert Crescents

(Pictured on page 7)

These mellow filbert cookies are liberally dusted with powdered sugar while they're still warm. They come out looking like snowy white crescent moons.

    ½ cup (¼ lb.) butter or margarine, softened
    ¼ cup powdered sugar
    ½ teaspoon vanilla
    1¼ cups all-purpose flour
    ⅛ teaspoon salt
    ½ cup finely chopped unblanched filberts or almonds
    Powdered sugar

In a large bowl, cream butter and the ¼ cup powdered sugar until fluffy. Beat in vanilla. In another bowl, combine flour and salt; gradually add flour mixture to creamed mixture, beating until well blended. Add nuts and stir to blend well.

For each cooky, roll dough into a ball about 1 inch in diameter, and roll between your palms into a strand about 2 inches long.

Place cookies on ungreased baking sheets and curve each into a crescent.

Bake in a 400° oven for about 10 minutes or until set but barely browned. Transfer cookies to racks with wax paper underneath. Sift powdered sugar generously over warm cookies. Let cool completely. Makes about 2 dozen cookies.

Date-Nut Brownies

Chopped dates and walnuts add texture, flavor, and nutritional value to these brownies. They're a great choice for picnicking with children.

2 ounces unsweetened
  chocolate
½ cup (¼ lb.) butter or margarine
1 cup sugar
2 eggs
1 teaspoon vanilla
½ cup all-purpose flour
¼ teaspoon *each* salt and baking
  powder
⅔ cup chopped pitted dates
1 cup chopped walnuts

In top of a double boiler, melt chocolate and butter over simmering water; set aside. In a small bowl, beat sugar and eggs until very light in color. Beat in chocolate mixture and vanilla.

In another bowl, combine flour, salt, and baking powder. Stir into batter, blending well. Add dates and nuts, stirring just until blended. Pour batter into a greased 9-inch square pan.

Bake in a 325° oven for 25 to 30 minutes or until a wooden pick inserted in center comes out clean. Let cool completely on a rack; cut into 24 bars. Makes 24 brownies.

Honey-Applesauce Cupcakes

(Pictured on page 34)

Down-to-earth cupcakes—honey-flavored and packed with dried fruits and nuts—take on a graceful new look when baked in brioche tins.

Chopped walnuts add a crunchy topping.

½ cup (¼ lb.) butter or margarine
1 cup honey
1 egg
1 teaspoon vanilla
1 cup whole wheat flour
1¼ cups all-purpose flour
1 teaspoon *each* baking soda
  and ground cinnamon
½ teaspoon *each* salt, ground
  cloves, and ground nutmeg
¼ teaspoon ground ginger
1 cup unsweetened applesauce
½ cup *each* raisins and chopped
  dried apricots
1 cup chopped pitted dates
⅔ cup coarsely chopped walnuts
⅓ cup finely chopped walnuts

Place butter in a bowl. Using an electric mixer, beat butter while gradually adding honey; beat in egg and vanilla. In a small bowl, stir together whole wheat flour, all-purpose flour, baking soda, cinnamon, salt, cloves, nutmeg, and ginger.

Add flour mixture to butter mixture alternately with applesauce, starting and ending with flour mixture. Stir in raisins, apricots, dates, and the ⅔ cup coarsely chopped nuts just until blended.

Spoon batter into well-greased 3-inch brioche tins or greased or paper-lined muffin pans, filling each three-quarters full. Sprinkle with the ⅓ cup finely chopped nuts.

Bake in a 350° oven for about 30 minutes or until tops spring back when lightly touched. Turn out onto racks to cool. Makes 20 cupcakes.

Almond Cake

(Pictured on page 47)

Hot lemon syrup soaks into this light, nutty sponge cake to give it extra moistness and flavor.

6 eggs, separated
1 cup sugar
½ cup all-purpose flour
1 teaspoon baking powder
¼ teaspoon almond extract
2 cups very finely ground
  blanched almonds
⅛ teaspoon *each* salt and cream
  of tartar
1 teaspoon grated lemon peel
  Lemon Syrup (recipe follows)
¾ cup finely chopped blanched
  almonds

In a large bowl, beat egg yolks until light; gradually add ½ cup of the sugar, beating until thick and lemon-colored. In a small bowl, combine flour and baking powder; stir into yolk mixture. Add almond extract and 1 cup of the ground almonds; mix just until nuts are well distributed.

In another bowl, beat egg whites until foamy; add salt and cream of tartar, beating until soft peaks form. Beat in remaining ½ cup sugar, a tablespoon at a time. Fold in lemon peel and remaining ground almonds.

Stir a quarter of the egg white mixture into egg yolk mixture until blended; then gently fold yolk mixture into remaining egg white mixture. Turn into a greased 9 by 13-inch baking pan.

Bake in a 350° oven for 20 to 25 minutes or until top springs back when lightly touched. Let cool in pan on a rack for 10 minutes. Meanwhile, prepare Lemon Syrup.

Cut cake into diamond-shaped pieces (make 4 length-

French Country Picnic

You can prepare everything a day ahead for this picnic à la française. Dine as the French do, starting with bacon-wrapped Country-style Pâté (page 19) accompanied by crusty baguettes and *cornichons*. For the entrée, plump, golden Roast Chicken with Herbs (page 49) served with Ratatouille (page 36) maintains the French accent, followed by a butter lettuce salad. A simple, subtly flavored pastry—Brandied Apricot Tart (page 84) with its sprinkling of slivered almonds—completes the elegant picnic.

wise cuts in cake, then cut diagonally 1¼ inches apart). Pour hot syrup over cake and sprinkle with chopped almonds. Let cool completely. Makes about 40 pieces.

Lemon Syrup. In a small pan, combine ¾ cup **sugar,** 3 tablespoons **lemon juice,** and ¼ cup **water.** Bring to a boil over high heat, and cook just until sugar is dissolved.

Almond Fudge Torte

(Pictured on page 83)

It looks like a pastry chef's pride and joy, but this rich, chewy torte is quite simple to prepare and easy to serve.

> 1 teaspoon instant coffee powder or granules
> 2 tablespoons hot water
> 4 ounces semisweet chocolate, melted
> 3 eggs, separated
> ½ cup (¼ lb.) butter or margarine
> ¾ cup sugar
> 2 ounces almond paste, crumbled or shredded
> ½ cup all-purpose flour
> Unsweetened cocoa
> Chocolate Glaze (recipe follows)

In a bowl, dissolve instant coffee in hot water; stir in melted chocolate. In another bowl, beat egg whites just until stiff, moist peaks form.

In a third bowl, cream butter and sugar until light and fluffy. Beat in almond paste, egg yolks, melted chocolate mixture, and flour. Fold in beaten egg whites, about a third at a time, just until blended. Spread in a greased and cocoa-dusted 8-inch round cake pan.

Bake in a 350° oven for

30 minutes or until lightly browned (*do not overbake*). Meanwhile, prepare Chocolate Glaze.

Let cake cool in pan on a rack for about 10 minutes; then turn out of pan to cool completely. Spread glaze over top and sides of cooled cake. Let stand until glaze hardens (2 to 4 hours at room temperature; 10 to 15 minutes in refrigerator). Serve at room temperature. Makes 10 servings.

Chocolate Glaze. In top of a double boiler, combine 4 ounces **semisweet chocolate** and 1 tablespoon **butter** or margarine. Stir over barely simmering water just until melted. Remove from heat and let cool, stirring occasionally, until slightly thickened.

Orange Fruitcake

(Pictured on page 83)

Less dense than traditional fruitcake, this fragrant version is generously studded with walnuts and dates.

> 1½ cups (¾ lb.) butter or margarine, softened
> 1½ cups granulated sugar
> 3 eggs
> 3¾ cups all-purpose flour
> 1½ teaspoons *each* baking powder and baking soda
> ¾ teaspoon salt
> 1½ cups buttermilk
> 1 cup *each* chopped pitted dates and chopped walnuts
> 1½ tablespoons grated orange peel
> 2 tablespoons all-purpose flour
> Powdered sugar

In a large bowl, cream butter and granulated sugar until light and fluffy. Add eggs, one at a time, beating well after

each addition. In another bowl, combine the 3¾ cups flour, baking powder, baking soda, and salt; add to creamed mixture alternately with buttermilk, beating after each addition.

In a small bowl, combine dates, nuts, and orange peel; dust with the 2 tablespoons flour, then stir into batter. Turn into a greased 12-cup bundt pan.

Bake in a 350° oven for 1 hour and 20 minutes or until a wooden pick inserted in center comes out clean. Let cool in pan for 10 minutes; then invert onto a rack to cool completely. Just before transporting, dust with powdered sugar. Makes 10 to 12 servings.

Picnic Chocolate Fondue

(Pictured on page 75)

Heat this easy fondue over glowing embers of the cooking fire, or take along a chafing dish.

> 16 ounces semisweet chocolate, coarsely chopped
> 1½ cups whipping cream
> One or more of the following for dipping: banana chunks, pineapple chunks, apple chunks, orange segments, strawberries, raspberries, kiwi fruit wedges, pound cake cubes, coconut macaroons

In a small pan over lowest possible heat, stir chocolate and cream constantly until chocolate is melted and well blended with cream. Let cool; pour into a jar to carry.

To serve, pour chocolate sauce into a small pan and warm over low coals. Offer forks to spear foods for dipping. Stir chocolate occasionally; if fire gets too hot, remove pan from heat. Makes 6 servings.

Portable Potables

Traditionalists may tell you that it's not a picnic without lemonade, or without iced tea, or without beer, but that's no reason to limit yourself when planning picnic beverages. You can be just as creative with liquid refreshment as with the rest of the menu—and maybe change the hearts of a few stubborn conformists while you're at it.

Wine punches

A refreshing wine punch is guaranteed to turn even the simplest picnic into a party. These drinks should be thoroughly chilled ahead of time and transported in a large prechilled thermos or thermal jug (see page 90); carbonated ingredients should be chilled and carried separately, to be added at the last minute. If your picnic plans include an ice chest, you can take along a bag of ice cubes and pour your beverage over ice just before serving. Garnishes can be taken in separate containers and added to each glass.

Bel Canto Punch. Chill 1 bottle (750 ml) **Riesling wine,** 2 cups **cranberry juice cocktail,** and ½ cup **Galliano liqueur.** Stir liquids together with 1 can (6 oz.) **frozen orange juice concentrate,** undiluted. Just before serving, stir in 1 bottle (28 oz.) chilled **ginger ale.** Makes about 10 cups.

Chilled Citrus Sangría. Combine 1 bottle (750 ml) **dry red wine,** 2 cups **fresh orange juice,** ½ cup *each* **fresh lime juice** and **fresh lemon juice,** and about ¼ cup **sugar;** cover and chill. Just before serving, stir in 2 cups chilled **sparkling water.** Garnish with **orange slices.** Makes about 8 cups.

French Kir. Chill 2 bottles (750 ml *each*) light, fruity **white wine.** Blend wine with ½ to 1 cup **crème de cassis** (amount depending on your taste). Before serving, place a twist of **lemon peel** in each glass. Makes about 7 cups.

Orange Vermouth Cooler. Chill 2 bottles (750 ml *each*) **dry vermouth** and let thaw 1 can (6 oz.) **frozen orange juice concentrate,** undiluted. Stir together

and add 3 cups cold **water.** To serve, garnish with **orange slices.** Makes about 11 cups.

Coolers

Besides being flavorful and fun, these cold drinks are real thirst-quenchers. With the exception of the Banana Fruit Slush, they should be packed and carried the same way as the wine punches (see above).

Banana Fruit Slush. In a large bowl, stir together 3 cups **water** and ¾ cup **sugar,** mixing until sugar is completely dissolved. Add 1 can (6 oz.) **frozen orange juice concentrate,** thawed, and 3 cups **pineapple-grapefruit juice;** mix well. In a blender or food processor, whirl 2 large **bananas** until puréed, then stir into juice mixture until well combined. Pour into a clean ½-gallon milk carton. Cover or tape carton shut; freeze for at least 24 hours or up to 6 months.

To serve, let punch thaw at room temperature for about 3 hours or until mixture is slushy. Stir in 1 bottle (32 oz.) **carbonated lemon-lime beverage,** breaking up frozen chunks of slush with a spoon; serve immediately. Makes 3 quarts.

Citrus Punch. Thaw and combine 1 can (6 oz.) *each* **frozen lemonade concentrate, frozen limeade concentrate,** and **frozen orange juice concentrate.** Just before serving, stir in 1 bottle (28 oz.) *each* chilled **sparkling water** and **ginger ale.** Garnish with **lime slices.** Makes about 9 cups.

Jasmine Tea Cooler. Place 12 **jasmine teabags** in a large container; pour 2 quarts **boiling water** over tea; cover and steep for 5 to 7 minutes. Discard teabags; add ¾ cup **sugar** and stir until sugar has dissolved. Let cool. Add 2 cups **milk** and chill. Makes about 10 cups.

Land and Sea. Chill and combine 6 cups (48 oz.) canned **chile-seasoned tomato cocktail** or Bloody Mary mix, 3 bottles (8 oz. *each*) canned **clam juice,** and 1 tablespoon **lemon juice.** Makes 9 cups.

Sparkling Water Mix-ups. To make these cooling drinks, chill your favorite variety of domestic or imported sparkling water and cold fruit juices separately. Then combine just before serving. If you like, garnish with fruit swizzle sticks made from cubes of watermelon, cantaloupe, honeydew, pineapple, and whole strawberries on thin bamboo skewers.

Tropical refresher: Two parts guava juice, guava nectar, or papaya juice with one part sparkling water.

Pomegranate sparkle: Two parts pomegranate juice with one part sparkling water, and a squeeze of lemon juice for each serving.

Mango lime splash: Mango juice with a splash of sparkling water and a squeeze of lime juice for each serving.

Citrus fizz: Equal parts sparkling water and lemonade or limeade (if using frozen concentrate, dilute with only half the amount of water called for on the can).

Warming treats

Drinks that are steaming hot and soothing are welcome warmers at a cold-weather picnic. Pack yours in a thermos that has been preheated with boiling water (see page 90). Serve in styrofoam cups if you don't want to carry mugs; *do not use wax-coated paper cups.*

Cranberry Glogg. In a pan, combine 4 cups **cranberry juice cocktail**, ¾ cup **orange juice**, ¼ cup **raisins**, 1 tablespoon **sugar**, 6 **cinnamon sticks**, and 18 **whole cloves.** Heat, uncovered, until simmering. Strain. To serve, garnish with **orange wedges.** Makes about 4 cups.

Hot Apricot Punch. In a pan, combine 3 cups **apricot nectar**, ½ cup **water**, 1 teaspoon **whole cloves**, and 2 tablespoons **sugar.** Bring to a boil; reduce heat and simmer gently, uncovered, for 5 minutes. Stir in 2 teaspoons **lemon juice** and ⅔ cup more **apricot nectar.** To serve, add a **cinnamon stick** to each serving. Makes about 4 cups.

Hot Gingered Lemonade. In a pan, combine 4 cups **water**; ¾ cup **frozen lemonade concentrate**, undiluted; and 3 to 4 tablespoons slivered **candied ginger.** Heat, uncovered, until simmering. To serve, stir well and garnish with **lemon slices.** Makes about 4 cups.

Latin Coffee. In a pan, combine 4 cups **whole milk**; ¾ cup **ground coffee**, fine or regular grind; and 2 tablespoons **sugar.** Heat, stirring constantly, until milk is scalding hot; *do not boil.* Pour mixture through a coffee filter or damp cloth (wrung dry) to remove grounds. Add ½ teaspoon **vanilla.** To serve, pass **sweetened whipped cream** to spoon into coffee, if desired (you'll need about ½ cup). Makes 4 cups.

Bracing libations

A touch of liqueur or spirits gives these hot drinks an extra fillip. Transport and serve them just as you would the hot beverages above.

Buttered Hot Cider. In a pan, combine 4 cups **apple cider**, 1 teaspoon **whole cloves**, 4 sticks **cinnamon**, ¼ teaspoon **ground nutmeg**, and 4 teaspoons **sugar.** Bring to a boil; reduce heat and simmer gently, uncovered, for 10 minutes. Stir in ⅔ cup **dark rum**; strain. To serve, top each portion with a pat (about 1 teaspoon) **butter.** Makes about 4 cups.

Coffee Bar Combinations. You take a thermos of hot coffee, a selection of flavorings, and a bowl of sweetened whipped cream. Then let your guests choose the ingredients for their own special coffee drinks. Allow about 1 ounce liquor for each cup of coffee.

Brazilian coffee: Coffee, crème de cacao, cinnamon stick, and whipped cream.

Irish coffee: Coffee, Irish whiskey, and whipped cream.

Mexican coffee: Coffee, coffee-flavored liqueur, cinnamon stick, and whipped cream.

Parisian coffee: Coffee, cognac, and whipped cream.

Hot Milk Punch. In a pan, scald 3¾ cups **milk.** Remove from heat and add 5 teaspoons **sugar**, 2 **cinnamon sticks**, 1½ teaspoons **vanilla**, and ½ cup light or dark **rum.** If desired, sprinkle each serving with **ground nutmeg.** Makes about 4 cups.

Chocolate Buttercream Cake

(Pictured on page 91)

Moist, rich chocolate cake is an ever-popular dessert, indoors or at a picnic. This one is frosted and filled with a fluffy chocolate buttercream.

¼ cup unsweetened cocoa
1 cup water
2 cups all-purpose flour
2 cups sugar
1 teaspoon baking soda
1 cup (½ lb.) butter or margarine, melted
2 eggs, lightly beaten
1 teaspoon vanilla
½ cup sour cream
   Chocolate Buttercream (recipe follows)
   Semisweet chocolate shavings

In a large bowl, blend cocoa and water. Sift flour, sugar, and baking soda into cocoa mixture and blend. Stir in butter, eggs, and vanilla. Using an electric mixer, beat for 2 minutes. Stir in sour cream. Pour into 2 greased and floured 8-inch round cake pans.

Bake in a 350° oven for 35 to 40 minutes or until cakes begin to pull away from sides of pans. Let cool in pans for 10 minutes; then invert on racks to cool completely.

Prepare Chocolate Buttercream and spread between layers and over top and sides of cake. Decorate with chocolate shavings. Makes 8 to 10 servings.

Chocolate Buttercream. Place ¾ cup (¼ lb. plus 4 tablespoons) **butter** or margarine and 1 cup **sugar** in a large bowl. Using an electric mixer, cream until light and fluffy. Add 4 ounces **unsweetened chocolate,** melted and cooled, and 2 teaspoons **vanilla;** beat well. Add 4 **eggs;** beat until light in color and thick (about 3 minutes). If mixture gets dark and runny from overbeating, chill; then beat again.

Lemon Cream Cheese Tarts

Cream cheese gives these tarts a rich, smooth creaminess that works in delicious counterpoint to their piquant lemon flavor. You can buy baked tart shells or make your own from your favorite pastry recipe.

3 eggs
¾ cup sugar
2 teaspoons grated lemon peel
½ cup lemon juice
1 large package (8 oz.) cream cheese, softened
10 baked 3-inch tart shells

In top of a double boiler, beat eggs until pale and frothy. Gradually beat in sugar until mixture is thickened and pale. Stir in lemon peel and juice. Cook over simmering water, stirring constantly, until mixture coats a spoon (about 5 minutes); remove from heat.

Cut cream cheese into 1-inch pieces; gradually beat into lemon mixture until well blended. Let cool; then spoon into baked tart shells. Cover loosely and refrigerate.

Transport in a cooler. Makes 10 tarts.

Pine Nut Tarts

(Pictured on page 31)

Buttery pine nut tarts are tiny but wonderfully rich.

½ cup (¼ lb.) butter or margarine, softened
1 small package (3 oz.) cream cheese, softened
1 tablespoon brandy (optional)
1¼ cups all-purpose flour
1 egg
¾ cup firmly packed light brown sugar
¼ teaspoon salt
1 tablespoon butter or margarine, melted
½ teaspoon vanilla
1 cup pine nuts
   About ¼ cup apricot jam

For pastry, beat the ½ cup butter and cream cheese in a large bowl until light and fluffy. Beat in brandy, if desired, then gradually mix in flour until dough is smooth. Shape into a roll and divide into 24 equal portions. Using your fingers, press each portion evenly over bottom and up sides of a 1½-inch muffin cup. Set aside.

For filling, beat egg in a large bowl until light; beat in sugar and salt, then add the 1 tablespoon melted butter and vanilla. Stir in pine nuts. Spoon filling evenly into pastry shells. Bake in a 350° oven for 30 minutes or until pastry and filling are well browned.

Heat apricot jam in a small pan over low heat; pour through a wire strainer. Brush tops of warm tarts with apricot glaze. Let cool completely in muffin cups.

To store or transport, place tarts in a single layer in a container at least 1 inch taller than tarts, so lid or foil covering is well above glaze. Store at room temperature for up to a week. Makes 2 dozen tarts.

English Garden Tea

When a splendid garden beckons, only the most magnificent table will do.
And what could be lovelier than this gracious English-style tea? Even the
sandwich selection—Watercress-Onion Sandwiches, Chicken-Almond Fingers,
and Dill Shrimp on Crackers (all on page 61)—lends a colorful complement to
the scene, along with flaky Cheese Twists (page 17). Sugar-dusted Orange
Fruitcake (page 79), wedges of rich Almond Fudge Torte (page 79), and pastel
mint wafers add a gentle finishing touch.

Fresh Raspberry Barquettes

(Pictured on page 55)

When fresh raspberries are in season, show them off in dainty little boat-shaped shells called barquettes.

Barquette Shells (recipe follows)
1½ cups raspberries
¼ cup sugar
2 tablespoons water
2 teaspoons cornstarch
½ teaspoon lemon juice
Dash of ground nutmeg
Whipped cream (optional)

Prepare Barquette Shells and let cool on a rack.

Place ½ cup of the raspberries in a blender or food processor. Add sugar and water; whirl until smooth. Pour mixture through a wire strainer into a medium-size pan; discard seeds.

Add cornstarch to berry mixture, stirring until smooth. Cook over medium-high heat, stirring constantly, until thickened and clear. Remove from heat and stir in lemon juice and nutmeg. Gently mix in remaining berries. Evenly spoon berry filling into barquette shells.

To transport, carefully place barquettes in a shallow pan or box. Transport whipped cream, if desired, in a cooler, and spoon onto barquettes just before serving. Makes 6 barquettes or 2 tarts.

Barquette Shells. In a small bowl, mix ½ cup **all-purpose flour,** 1 tablespoon **powdered sugar,** and a dash of **salt.** With a pastry blender or 2 knives, cut 3 tablespoons firm **butter** or margarine into flour mixture until it resembles fine crumbs.

Stir in 1 **egg yolk;** then use your hands to press dough together.

Divide pastry into 6 equal portions. Press each portion evenly into a barquette pan about 4½ inches long and ½ inch deep. (Or divide pastry into 2 equal portions and press each into a tart pan about 4 inches in diameter and 1 inch deep.) With a fork, prick bottom and sides all over.

Bake in a 425° oven for 8 to 10 minutes or until golden brown. Let cool in pans for about 10 minutes; then, protecting your hands, tip shells out of pans and set on a rack to cool completely. Makes 6 barquette shells or two 4-inch tart shells.

Crunchy Walnut Pie or Tarts

If ever there was an ideal picnic pie, this is it. It's simple to make, it's firm-textured enough for easy slicing and eating, and it tastes best if baked a day ahead and allowed to stand. If you prefer, make individual tarts as directed below.

Pastry for a single-crust 9-inch pie
3 eggs
½ cup firmly packed brown sugar
1 cup light corn syrup
¼ teaspoon salt
1 teaspoon *each* ground cinnamon and vanilla
4 tablespoons butter or margarine, melted
1 cup broken walnuts or walnut halves

Roll out pastry and fit loosely into a pie pan; crimp or flute edge decoratively.

In a bowl, beat eggs until light and frothy. Beat in brown sugar, corn syrup, salt, cinnamon, vanilla, and butter. Stir in nuts. Pour mixture into pastry shell.

Place pie on lowest shelf of a 375° oven and bake for about 50 minutes or until filling jiggles only slightly when dish is gently shaken. Let cool on a rack for at least 2 hours. When completely cool, cover with foil. Store at room temperature. Makes 6 to 8 servings.

Walnut Tarts. Roll out **pastry** for a single-crust 9-inch pie to a thickness of ⅛ inch. Cut eight 4½-inch circles and press each pastry circle into a 3-inch brioche tin.

In a bowl, beat 1 **egg** until light and frothy. Beat in 2½ tablespoons firmly packed **brown sugar,** ⅓ cup **light corn syrup,** pinch of **salt,** ¼ teaspoon **ground cinnamon,** ½ teaspoon **vanilla,** and 1½ tablespoons **butter** or margarine, melted. Distribute ⅓ cup coarsely chopped **walnuts** evenly in pastry shells; then carefully pour in filling.

Place filled shells on a baking sheet and bake in a 400° oven for 20 minutes or until tops spring back when lightly touched. Let cool on racks for 30 minutes. Run a sharp knife around edge of each tart to loosen pastry; then place your hand over tart and invert tin to let tart slip out. Let cool completely on racks. Makes 8 tarts.

Brandied Apricot Tart

(Pictured on page 78)

You don't need many ingredients for this brandy-laced fruit tart; it goes together quickly, yet the final effect is elegant. After cooling, the tart can be covered lightly with plastic wrap and packed in a shallow box for transporting.

- 1 sheet (half a 17¼-oz. package) frozen puff pastry, thawed
- ¾ cup apricot jam
- 2 tablespoons apricot brandy or apricot-flavored liqueur
- 4 cans (17 oz. *each*) peeled whole apricots, drained, cut in half, and pitted
- 2 tablespoons slivered almonds

On a lightly floured board, roll out pastry to fit a 10-inch tart pan. Place pastry in pan, trim edges, and prick all over with a fork. Set a circle of foil inside pastry shell and partially fill with dry beans or rice. Bake, uncovered, in a 400° oven for 20 to 25 minutes or until crust is a light golden color. Let cool slightly; then lift off foil and beans.

In a small pan over low heat, combine jam and brandy; heat until jam melts to form a glaze. Brush glaze lightly over bottom of pastry shell. Arrange a layer of apricots, cut side down, in pastry shell and brush with glaze. Cover with another layer of apricots, arranged decoratively cut side down, and glaze heavily. Sprinkle with almonds and glaze again.

Reduce oven temperature to 325°, return tart to oven, and bake, uncovered, for 10 more minutes or until crust is slightly darker and apricots are heated through. Let cool on a rack. Makes 6 to 8 servings.

Glazed Apple Pie Bars

Here's a change of pace for apple-pie lovers. It's a double-crust pie that's rectangular, made on a baking sheet, and covered with nuts and a sweet lemon glaze.

- 12 medium-size cooking apples, peeled, cored, and thinly sliced
- ¾ cup coarsely chopped walnuts
- 2 cups granulated sugar
- 2 teaspoons ground cinnamon
- ⅛ teaspoon ground nutmeg
- 2 teaspoons lemon juice
  Pastry for 2 double-crust 9-inch pies
- 4 tablespoons butter or margarine
- 3 tablespoons lemon juice
- 1½ cups powdered sugar
- ½ cup finely chopped walnuts

In a bowl, combine apples, the ¾ cup coarsely chopped walnuts, granulated sugar, cinnamon, nutmeg, and the 2 teaspoons lemon juice.

Roll out half the pastry to fit an 11 by 15-inch rimmed baking sheet. Place pastry on baking sheet and cover with apple filling to within ½ inch of edge; dot with butter. Roll out remaining pastry and place over apples. Turn edges of bottom pastry over top and flute or pinch edges to seal; prick top in several places.

Bake in a 350° oven for 1 hour or until apples are tender when pierced with a wooden pick and crust is golden brown.

Meanwhile, in a bowl, mix the 3 tablespoons lemon juice with powdered sugar. Spread icing over hot pastry; sprinkle with the ½ cup finely chopped walnuts. Let cool; then cut into bars. Makes 24 bars.

Poppy Seed Loaf

(Pictured on page 86)

The rich sweetness of molasses and the crunch of poppy seeds are featured in this moist bread.

- 4 eggs
- 1 cup salad oil
- ½ cup light or dark molasses
- 1¾ cups firmly packed brown sugar
- 1½ cups *each* all-purpose flour and whole wheat flour
- 1 teaspoon baking soda
- 1 can (13 oz.) evaporated milk
- ½ cup poppy seeds
- 1 teaspoon vanilla
  Whipped cream (optional)

In a large bowl, beat eggs, oil, molasses, and brown sugar until smooth. In another bowl, combine all-purpose flour, whole wheat flour, and baking soda; add to molasses mixture alternately with milk, beating well after each addition.

Reserve 2 tablespoons of the poppy seeds; stir remaining poppy seeds and vanilla into batter. Turn batter into 2 greased 9 by 5-inch loaf pans; sprinkle with reserved seeds.

Bake in a 325° oven for 50 to 60 minutes or until a wooden pick inserted in center comes out clean. Let cool slightly in pans; then turn out onto racks to cool completely. To serve, top each slice with whipped cream, if desired (transport whipped cream in a cooler). Makes 2 loaves.

Strawberry Ice Cream

(Pictured on page 91)

Re-create a bit of old-time Americana by making ice

Harvest Picnic

Terra cotta containers not only carry and serve these picnic foods, but also add a rustic, earthy quality. The crust of German Vegetable Pie (page 57) conceals a dense and savory filling. With Terrine of Pork, Veal & Ham (page 21), crusty bread, and cherry tomatoes, it makes a substantial meal. Poppy Seed Loaf (page 85) and ripe pears make a wholesome dessert.

cream at your picnic. Be sure there's a large group of people around—you'll need helpers, both for hand-cranking and for consuming the abundant fruits of your labor!

- 3 eggs
- ½ teaspoon salt
- 1¾ cups sugar
- 3 cups *each* milk and half-and-half (light cream)
- 1 tablespoon vanilla
- 4 baskets strawberries
- 2 tablespoons lemon juice
-   Ice
-   Rock salt

In a bowl, beat eggs until foamy. Beat in salt and 1 cup of the sugar. Scald milk in a 2-quart pan over medium-high heat. Beat a little of the scalded milk into egg mixture; then return mixture to pan, stirring. Reduce heat to low and cook, stirring constantly, until custard coats a spoon (6 to 8 minutes). *Do not* let custard boil. Remove from heat and let cool. Stir in half-and-half and vanilla. Pour into a container, cover tightly, and refrigerate until well chilled.

Hull berries (you should have 6 cups), and crush. Stir in lemon juice and remaining ¾ cup sugar. Refrigerate until well chilled.

Transport custard, berry mixture, and ice in a cooler. When ready to process, assemble hand-crank ice cream freezer (or an electric one, if you have an outlet) according to manufacturer's instructions. Pour custard into cylinder, cover, and surround cylinder with layers of ice and rock salt, using 4 parts ice to 1 part salt.

Begin cranking (or start motor). When custard begins to thicken, add berry mixture. When hand-cranking becomes difficult (or motor labors or stalls), ice cream is ready. Serve immediately, or remove dasher, replace cover on cylinder, and leave ice cream in freezer to ripen (drain brine and repack freezer with ice to keep ice cream colder). Makes 1 gallon.

Flavored Fruits

Combining seasonal fruits with wine or liqueur is a wonderful way to present a special dessert and still enjoy natural fruit flavor. Here are four easy ideas to inspire you.

Strawberries Grand Marnier. Hull 1 or 2 baskets firm, ripe **strawberries,** leaving berries whole. Place in a bowl and sprinkle with **sugar** and **Grand Marnier** to taste. Chill well. Makes 2 to 6 servings.

Pineapple with Grapefruit & Kirsch. In a bowl, combine 2 cups fresh **pineapple** chunks with 1 cup **grapefruit** sections, white membrane removed. Sprinkle 1 tablespoon **kirsch** over fruit and mix lightly. Refrigerate for about an hour. Makes 4 or 5 servings.

Pears Baked in Wine. Insert 1 whole clove into blossom end of each of 4 whole, unpeeled **pears** (including stems). Arrange pears in a deep casserole (fruit may be placed on sides); add 1 cup **red wine,** ½ cup **water,** and ½ cup **sugar.** Cover and bake in a 400° oven for about 30 minutes, basting occasionally. Uncover and continue baking for 15 to 20 more minutes or until pears are very tender; baste frequently. Serve at room temperature or refrigerate and serve cold. Makes 4 servings

Spiced Peaches in Wine. Pour ½ cup **burgundy** into a small pan and add 2 tablespoons **powdered sugar,** 1 whole **cinnamon stick,** 1 teaspoon **lemon juice,** and peel of half a **lemon.** Bring to a boil; reduce heat and simmer, uncovered, for 3 minutes. Pour hot syrup over 3 peeled, halved, and pitted **peaches.** Let stand for at least 2 hours; serve at room temperature. Makes 3 to 6 servings.

Sherried Cream with Fruit

This elegant, sherry-flavored custard sauce is meant for fruit at its peak. Use only fruit that's very fresh and completely ripe for this show-off dessert.

- ⅓ cup sugar
- 2 tablespoons cornstarch
- ⅛ teaspoon salt
- 2 cups milk
- ¼ cup cream sherry or apple juice
- 2 egg yolks, lightly beaten
- 2 tablespoons butter or margarine
- 1 teaspoon vanilla
-   About 1½ cups seedless red or green grapes, diced fresh pineapple, or sliced nectarines

In a 2-quart pan, stir together sugar, cornstarch, and salt. Gradually stir in milk and sherry until well blended. Place pan over medium heat and cook, stirring constantly, until mixture boils; continue to boil for 1 minute. Remove from heat.

Stir part of hot sauce into beaten yolks; transfer yolk mixture to pan and cook for 30 seconds. Remove from heat and stir in butter and vanilla until butter is melted. Let cool slightly; then cover loosely and refrigerate.

Transport in a cooler. To serve, spoon custard sauce over each serving of fruit. Makes 4 servings.

Picnic Know-how

Planning and orchestrating the perfect picnic

There's no question about it— organization is the key to successful picnicking. Even a spur-of-the-moment picnic should be a well-planned one, lest you find yourself sitting on wet grass, slapping mosquitos, eating squashed sandwiches, and wishing you'd remembered the bottle opener.

To avoid such picnic nightmares, plan your excursion carefully. How will you pack your food to keep it fresh, insulated, and intact? What equipment and utensils will you need for eating, setting up, and cooking out? Make a checklist so you don't forget anything, and keep a copy with your picnic gear to smooth the way for upcoming picnics.

You can buy plenty of paraphernalia for dining easily and comfortably in the great outdoors. Combine it with useful household articles, a little ingenuity, and some basic know-how, and your picnics will be relaxed, pleasurable experiences.

Picnic Paraphernalia

Picnic equipment can be as simple as paper plates in a brown bag, or as elegant as a wicker hamper specially fitted with flatware and china. Picnic enthusiasts tend to accumulate equipment over a period of time, and to collect the supplies that suit the kind of picnicking they do most often.

Let's consider the paraphernalia you can use to transport, insulate, cook, and eat your picnic feast—whether it's a backpacker's basic lunch for two or a feast for eight.

For transporting food

If you're not traveling far and your provisions aren't perishable, you can carry your picnic in a brown grocery bag—that's part of the casual spirit of picnicking. But why rough it, if that's not your style? Other options offer you more packing space, easier carrying, better insulation, or simply more charm than any paper bag ever could.

Baskets. Import stores, gourmet shops, hardware stores, and gift emporiums carry baskets of straw, wicker, bamboo, woven rope, and even vinyl-covered steel wire. These baskets may be open or have hinged lids, and they may be lined with gingham or other gaily colored fabric. They may come empty or be outfitted with removable trays and/or picnic gear such as plastic plates, cups, flatware, and cloth napkins. The ultimate is an English picnic hamper—a large, costly wicker chest, its inside surfaces fitted with straps that hold a complete table service for several people.

When you're shopping for a picnic basket, look for a sturdy,

roomy one. If it has handles, they should be strong and durable, especially on larger models. Whether or not the basket should have a lid is a matter of personal preference. A lid can provide a handy cutting or serving surface, but food can be covered just as well in an open basket if you line the basket with a pretty tablecloth and then fold it over the contents when the basket is full. Try this technique, too, with a brightly colored plastic laundry basket and a tablecloth in harmonizing colors.

Coolers. For perishable picnic foods, a cooler (ice chest) is a better choice than a basket. Foods that spoil quickly, such as meats, fish, mayonnaise, and most dairy products, *must* be kept cool to prevent bacterial growth and the possibility of food poisoning (see page 20). Even inexpensive styrofoam coolers can keep foods fresh and cool for hours, though they're less durable than insulated metal or heavy-duty plastic models.

When purchasing a cooler, look for sturdiness; strong, easy-to-hold handles; and tight lids that lock in place. Many coolers have lids that are hinged so they don't blow away or get lost, or that are indented to hold glasses. Some contain trays that keep food away from melting ice. Another useful feature is a leakproof drain.

Besides the large chest-style coolers, you'll find newer, lighter models that are carried by one handle at the top, and smaller versions that you can carry with a strap.

For more information on coolers, see "For keeping foods hot or cold" on page 90.

Bags. Designed especially for carrying foods and beverages and keeping them cool, "refrigerator bags" are usually

insulated with fiberglass, covered and lined with vinyl, and fitted with wraparound handles and a zipper that allows the flat top to be opened on three sides. We've also seen refrigerator bags with canvas exteriors rather than plastic.

You can use refrigerator bags for hot foods, too—they'll maintain a given temperature for several hours. If hot food is in a very hot container—particularly glass or metal—you'd be wise to protect the vinyl bag from heat by wrapping the container in newspaper first.

Nylon or canvas duffle bags used for sailing and for carrying athletic equipment also make good picnic carry-alls. They're roomy and strong, with sturdy straps and reinforced bottoms. Fishing tackle bags are useful too.

You might also think about using old luggage for picnic toting. Anything from a small carry-on airplane bag to a large, lightweight suitcase may do beautifully. Backpacks are convenient carriers, too. A light day pack works well for small meals, a larger frame pack for more ambitious picnic projects.

Any kind of cloth, straw, or woven bag may also fill your needs. Or you can simply wrap your picnic in a tablecloth or other ground cover, bring the corners together, and knot them, like a Japanese *furoshiki*. You can also use this technique with oversize cloth napkins for individual picnic meals.

For keeping foods hot or cold

Equipment for keeping picnic foods at the right temperature has reached new heights of sophistication. Thermal containers come in many shapes, sizes, and materials, and range from inexpensive plastic models with plastic inner linings to more expensive and heavier steel versions with glass inner linings. (Glass keeps liquid at a desired temperature for a longer time.) Some containers are even made of unglazed pottery; you soak them in water before using, and evaporation keeps the contents cool. Wide-mouthed thermal containers are useful for carrying chunky foods.

Large insulated jugs or vacuum bottles are excellent for serving beverages to a crowd. Pump-action jugs with spigots near the top dispense liquid when the top of the jug is pressed, avoiding the necessity of tipping the jug as it empties. Most of these pump-action jugs work best with clear, thin liquids such as coffee, iced tea, and fruit punch. They do not work as well for thicker liquids such as milk and soup.

The large collapsible water jugs found in sporting goods stores are a good option for cold beverages. Some have openings wide enough for ice cubes; or, if the directions state that the jug can be frozen, you can freeze a layer of ice inside the jug before you add the liquid.

To keep food hot, it's possible to buy insulated casseroles or casseroles with a snap-on quilted cosy. But you can insulate any hot dish—such as a Dutch oven or other hot casserole—for several hours by wrapping it in heavy foil and then in 6 to 8 layers of newspaper, tying it with string, and carrying it in a closed box or refrigerator bag. This technique can also be applied to hot sandwiches or turnovers or any other hot food—just remember to add a double layer of paper toweling under the foil to absorb steam if you're carrying something with a flaky pastry crust.

For keeping the chill on foods in a cooler, you have several alternatives. One is a layer of ice on the bottom of the cooler; another is blocks of ice made by freezing water inside clean milk cartons. Dry ice also can be an effective refrigerant; always wrap it in paper before using, and place it on *top* of the foods you want to remain cold.

Easiest of all, perhaps, are the containers of artificial refrigerant that can be purchased in hardware or sporting goods stores. You freeze these plastic-coated blocks of chemical gel and then place them on top of the food in your cooler. They are compact, reusable, and mess-free.

Experienced picnickers have many tips for keeping food and drink at desired temperatures. We share some of them here with you:

• Keep in mind that the function of a cooler is to *keep* foods cool—not to *make* them cool. Chill the food thoroughly before you put it in the cooler.

• Prechill your cooler before packing it by filling the cooler with ice or ice water and allowing it to stand for an hour.

• Prechill or preheat thermal containers. To prechill, fill the container with ice water, cap and let stand for 10 minutes; or place the open container in the refrigerator for an hour. To preheat, fill with boiling water; then cap and let stand while you prepare the hot beverage.

• Remember that the bottom of your cooler will be the coldest place, and pack accordingly. Drinks can be packed in the ice on the bottom; perishables should be kept directly over the ice.

• For best cooling, leave room for air to circulate inside the cooler; try not to fill every nook and cranny when you pack.

• When you arrive at your picnic site, find a shady place for the cooler. If possible, cover it with a blanket or towel. Open it only when necessary, and never allow a cooler to stand open if perishable food is inside.

For cooking at the picnic

Several types of outdoor cooking apparatus are portable and simple to use away from home. For barbecuing, consider a hibachi; these small, portable barbecue units are easily disassembled and carried. Some even fold in half and slide into a carrying case. They're inexpensive and need only a few coals for cooking.

Some small-model basic barbecue units are designed for portability and table-top use. If you don't want to carry charcoal briquets, choose a gas-fueled model. Portable barbecues are rugged and compact; their legs may be removable or may fold to become handles.

If you're barbecuing with charcoal, don't forget liquid starter, unless you have pretreated briquets. Take long-handled tongs, forks, and spatulas, as well as potholders and plenty of fireplace matches.

Outdoor cooking is also possible on a campstove. These stoves come in dozens of models, but if you base your choice on stove size and fuel variety, you can select the most suitable stove for your picnicking needs.

Fourth of July Potluck Supper

This traditional family picnic for the Fourth of July can easily satisfy lots of hearty appetites. What's difficult is deciding what to eat, starting with the two entrées, Crusty Parmesan Chicken (page 51) and barbecued cheeseburgers with all the fixings. Side dishes offer even more of a challenge. Choose—if you can—from among Parsley Potato Salad (page 32), Mushroom-Artichoke Salad (page 29), Chili-spiced Bean Salad (page 32), and deviled eggs. Dessert is easy—just serve thick wedges of Chocolate Buttercream Cake (page 82) with scoops of homemade Strawberry Ice Cream (page 85).

Choices in tableware

Even if you've made an effort to provide lots of finger food, you'll probably need some eating equipment at your picnic. You may want to create an atmosphere of outdoor luxury and take your china or stoneware plates from home (well wrapped, of course). Most picnics, though, are better suited to more rugged supplies. Colorful plastic plates that stack for easy carrying are practical picnic choices, as are plates of light enameled steel.

If you prefer disposable tableware, choose paper plates, available in many sturdy versions. Some are divided into sections to keep foods separated. If you want extra support for your paper plates, wicker paper-plate holders can provide the needed reinforcement.

Grandmother might shudder at the thought of her silverware at a picnic table miles from home, but she'd certainly approve of stainless steel utensils, either your everyday tableware or an inexpensive set bought especially for picnic use. Or you can opt for heavy-duty plastic tableware that doesn't chip or break and is dishwasher-safe; you can use it again and again.

For drinking, let your menu determine the glasses you choose. Wine aficionados may decide it's worth the effort to wrap and carry real wine glasses rather than use plastic or paper cups, though these

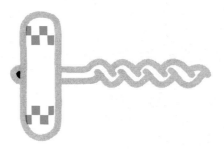

are usually fine for other cold drinks. For hot beverages, use styrofoam cups if you don't want to carry mugs.

Informal cloth napkins provide a nice touch and are less likely to blow away than their paper counterparts. If you prefer the disposable variety, be sure to take plenty of them.

Handy odds and ends

A list of other needed paraphernalia might include these: a can opener, bottle opener, reliable corkscrew, salt shaker, pepper mill, sharp knife, cutting board, serving utensils, garbage bags, and premoistened towelettes.

Perfect Packing

After you've decided on your menu and supplies, you'll want to pack your picnic efficiently. Here we share some tips that will help prevent spoiled food, broken dishes, and spills, and will help avoid confusion when it's time to serve the food.

● Don't take too much food. The well-organized picnic basket contains enough for each person and very little excess. It is inconvenient to carry leftovers home. If they're perishable, they should be thrown out anyway; they probably won't be fresh enough to be taken home and eaten later.

● In a picnic basket, pack the things you'll need last at the bottom and those you'll need first at the top. This way, you can unpack the picnic in its natural sequence without having to dig for things. Set fragile dishes on top of sturdy items to reduce the risk of chipping, cracking, or breaking the dishes. And of course any fragile foods that aren't in

protective containers must be given the same consideration. If using a cooler, follow the sequence rule as nearly as possible, but put perishables and cold drinks near the bottom of the chest to keep them cool.

● In a cooler with ice at the bottom, you can nestle bottles, cans, and sealed cartons right into the ice. But for sandwiches, meats, salads, and other foods you want to keep cool but away from moisture, it's helpful to have a shelf resting inside the cooler above the ice level. If your cooler doesn't have such a shelf, you can easily make one. Many styrofoam coolers have a ledge on which a shelf can rest; others have tapered sides that allow a shelf to be wedged in place. Measure the cooler carefully and then cut a piece of lightweight ⅛-inch perforated hardboard to fit the inside of the cooler. You can also cut holes in it to fit over bottles and cartons that stand upright, and the shelf will prevent them from tipping over. Drill a ¾-inch finger hole so you can lift the shelf out easily.

● Foods that can leak or spill should be packed in jars with tightly screwed-on lids or in containers that can be sealed shut with snap-on tops. Use masking tape to keep lids in place if there's any doubt. When wrapping foods, remember that aluminum foil stays in place better than plastic wrap; it's also a better insulator. If you can't see foods inside their wrapping or containers, label them for easy identification.

● Flatware can be grouped by place setting and wrapped in individual napkins or kept together with rubber bands. This makes the picnic basket neater and simplifies serving. Cloth napkins are also useful as protective wrappers for glassware.

Setting the Scene

Picture an expanse of grass, a gently sloping sand dune, or a grove of trees. Inviting, certainly—but maybe not as comfortable for picnicking as you might like. Your job, then, is to *make* it comfortable with amenities brought from home.

Beneath your banquet

If wet grass, sandy feet, and insects don't faze you, you may need no more than a tablecloth on which to spread your picnic.

If you want a picnic cloth with a wipe-clean surface, select a vinyl tablecloth or oilcloth in a bright color or bold design.

Bright beach towels are attractive and provide a little more padding than table-cloths—an advantage if you're picnicking on hard ground. Woven mats that roll up for easy under-the-arm carrying make interesting background textures for food; look for them in Oriental import shops.

Colorful sheets, old or inexpensive bedspreads or blankets, and tarpaulins are also possibilities.

To solve the blow-away problem with picnic cloths, sew a flap onto the back side of each corner of your cloth, forming a small pocket at each corner. When you spread the cloth, insert stones, sand, or fishing weights in each pocket.

Chairs and tables

If you don't want to sit on the ground, you can take along lightweight chairs. Large, soft cushions may be comfortable and romantic, but they are also bulky. Folding chairs and camp stools can be toted more easily. The aluminum-frame canoe chairs sold in sporting goods stores are lightweight and convenient to carry, and provide a back to lean against.

It can be difficult to carry a table to a picnic, but if you're eating near your car, you can take almost anything. Old card tables work well, and their legs can be cut down if you just want a level, clean surface for food and don't mind sitting on the ground.

For table-and-chair picnickers, folding camp tables provide a perfect solution. They fold into a conveniently carried rectangle, unfold into a table-and-chair unit for four, and need not rest on a level surface to stand securely.

For a final, festive note, take along a beach umbrella. It can be an effective wind-break and sun screen for your picnic food and guests. Some umbrellas clamp onto a chair back or table edge.

Picnic Etiquette

Certain rules are basic to the art of picnicking. Most of them are based on a regard for the environment and for the safety, comfort, and rights of others. A good picnicker is not only someone who can create a delightful *alfresco* meal, but one who observes principles of picnic etiquette.

- Don't trespass on private property. If you want to picnic on private land, get permission first. If you plan to use public land, check ahead. You may need to reserve a space or pay a fee for the use of picnic tables, barbecue pits, or other facilities.

- Observe all regulations pertaining to the site you've chosen. This may include rules about fire permits (often necessary for campstoves as well as open fires), pets, swimming, fishing, and gathering flowers or wild fruits and vegetables.

- Be safety conscious. Take along a first-aid kit in case of burns, cuts, bites, or other accidents. You may also want to include such items as insect repellent, motion-sickness pills, tweezers (for splinters), and sunscreen or suntan lotion. If poison oak or poison ivy grows in your area, inform guests and make sure they know how to identify it. Also warn of any danger from snakes, bears, or other animals, and know what to do if you encounter them.

- Be conscientious about fire safety; cooking fires should be watched at all times and thoroughly extinguished when the picnic is over.

- Caution members of your party, especially children, against drinking from streams or eating wild berries, mush-rooms, or other plants that may not be safe. Make sure children stay close to the picnic site so they don't get lost or wander into hazardous areas.

- Keep the noise level down if you're picnicking near other people. Blaring radios and screaming children will not endear you to your fellow picnickers.

- Clean up thoroughly after your picnic. Throw away *all* trash in appropriate containers, or take it home. Make sure that extinguished coals or wood from fires are well buried. In short, leave the picnic site as you would want to find it.

Tailgate Deli Picnic

Picnic in casual elegance from the tailgate of your car (even if it's a more recent model) with this purchased deli-style menu. Smother fresh bagels in cream cheese and top with thin slices of smoked salmon; layer New York-style corn rye bread with sliced pastrami and Swiss cheese. For crunch, take along kosher dill pickles and cole slaw. Cream cheese doubles as a dessert spread on crisp ginger cookies; each wafer is then topped with a few perfect raspberries.

Index

Metric Conversion Table

To change	To	Multiply by
ounces (oz.)	grams (g)	28
pounds (lbs.)	kilograms (kg)	0.45
teaspoons	milliliters (ml)	5
tablespoons	milliliters (ml)	15
fluid ounces (fl. oz.)	milliliters (ml)	30
cups	liters (l)	0.24
pints (pt.)	liters (l)	0.47
quarts (qt.)	liters (l)	0.95
gallons (gal.)	liters (l)	3.8
Fahrenheit temperature (°F)	Celsius temperature (°C)	5/9 after subtracting 32